# CONTENTED COWS

## *Give Better Milk*

THE PLAIN TRUTH ABOUT EMPLOYEE RELATIONS
AND YOUR BOTTOM LINE

*By*

**Bill Catlette**

*&*

**Richard Hadden**

*9/17/01*
*Good luck &*
*Godspeed!*
*Bill Catlette*

Saltillo Press
*Germantown, Tennessee*

Permissions Department
Saltillo Press
7608 Poplar Pike
Germantown, TN 38138
(901) 756–4661
E-Mail: WillifordS@aol.com

*Publisher:* Steve Williford
*Editor-in-Chief:* Robbin Brent
*Associate Editor:* Trent Booker
*Cover Design:* Patterson Graham Design Group
*Interior Design:* Electronic Publishing Services, Inc., Tennessee

**Library of Congress Cataloging-in-Publication Data**

Catlette, Bill and Hadden, Richard.
    Contented Cows Give Better Milk: the plain truth about employee relations and your bottom line / Bill Catlette and Richard Hadden.
        p.   cm.
ISBN 1-890-651-10-9
1. Business     I. Title

Printed on approved acid-free paper
1 2 3 4 5 6 7 8 9 10

Dedication

To Mary and Christine

# Contents

# FOREWORD

Few would disagree that treating people right, whatever right means, is generally good business practice. After all, it is one of the few truly timeless principles of life itself. But in the world of business, as in life, how many organizations and leaders actually manage to operationalize that premise consistently—day in and day out, rain or shine? Is it because we're unable to grasp the concept? Hardly. The concept is simple as dirt. Do we lack the authority (individually), or maybe the funds (institutionally) to make it happen? Nope. Neither has anything to do with it.

Rather, despite our (and we do mean our) best intentions, we seem to get derailed by a blizzard of fads on the one hand, and near-term urgencies cross-dressed as strategic imperatives on the other. While we have yet to see anyone proclaiming that treating people badly is somehow good for business, we have yet to see a compelling, unemotional case made for the converse. In a similar vein, business bookshelves and boardrooms are cluttered with the all too predictable (and easy) prescriptions for empowerment, teaming, restructuring, and the like.

So this book is an effort to establish a bottom-line-based case for the principle that if you treat people right, you'll make more money, period. It represents a challenge to each of us. Because once a clear and compelling reason to do something is established, and the path is made just a little brighter, it all comes down to a personal decision. You either act or you don't.

Throughout the book, we have used a somewhat conversational tone ... a little too conversational to suit our editor. But we've hung with it for a reason, actually two of them. First, neither of us especially enjoys being lectured to or preached at and we suspect you feel the same way. Second, it is about to become abundantly clear that in each of our cases, our first avocation is not as a writer, but as a business person for whom the lessons and advice contained on these pages are as relevant as for any reader.

Titling a book is not easy. That was particularly true in this case. We were told that the book's essence must be conveyed in six or fewer words, and the clearer and more memorable, the better. To us, the use of the cow as a metaphor seemed highly appropriate. To understand the metaphor as we intend it, one should focus not on any unflattering physical characteristics which may be attributed to members of the bovine species, but on the fact that for hundreds, perhaps thousands of years, cows have served as productive life partners and indeed as measures of wealth and stature. For those who might be put off by a comparison of working people to cows, get over it.

Though we felt strongly about it, we struggled with the *contented* part, on two fronts. Our first concern was that some might confuse the term *contented* with adjectives like happy, carefree, giddy, kinder-gentler, etc. If you need to, look it up. That's not what it means ... anything but. It represents *exactly* what we mean to convey: *A person's degree of satisfaction with their work situation is entirely and directly related to their output.*

The second problem had to do with the expression *Contented Cows* which, it turns out, is a trademarked expression, the rights to which are owned by Nestle. No fewer than four attorney friends (How's that for an oxymoron.) told us in no uncertain terms, "Don't even think about it." So we went ahead and asked anyhow. We are eternally grateful to the folks at Nestle for their understanding, support, and having the good heart to say "yes."

With the rationale and the path clear, let's proceed.

# ACKNOWLEDGMENTS

This book was an ongoing project for better than two years. In the course of researching, writing, and publishing it, we relied on the efforts of many. We are, and will continue to be, grateful for their assistance. Here are just a few of the people without whose help we couldn't have done it. ...

Our publisher and partner, Steve Williford, whose gracious good humor is as beneficial as his literary and publishing skills.

Our editor-in-chief, Robbin Brent, who pushed, cajoled, worked tirelessly, and neither offered nor accepted any excuses. Associate editor, Trent Booker, who wordsmithed, gracefully put up with our foibles, and voluntarily learned more about cows than any non-dairy farmer should have to.

Pat Patterson, who designed the most outrageous cover we've seen on a business book, and Rick Soldin, who took a pile of stuff and made it look like a real book.

Brad Ziemba, who spent several days in the University of Memphis library checking and re-checking the numbers, and Karey Bakker, who interviewed many of the sources within the companies we've featured.

Wayne Morris, Jane Lemmon, Beth Irvine, and Tom Ladet, who spent countless hours reading the manuscript for us, and who cared enough to tell us the truth.

Corporate chieftains Truett Cathy, David Graham, Dennis LeStrange, Sal Quadrino, Dennis Spina, and Mike Smith, who supported our effort with their ideas, their good example, and their time.

For sharing information about their respective companies, we thank Heather Jardim of Kingston Technologies, Betty Kahn of Crate & Barrel, Scott Mayson and Jerry Johnston of Chick-fil-A, David Russo of SAS Institute, and Valerie Wagner of Starbucks Coffee ... as well as so many others we've met informally in our travels, and who were kind enough to answer our questions.

We also thank fellow members of SHRM, who helped us define and refine the lists of *Contented* and *Common Cows*.

Tom Peters, who, without even knowing it, served as an inspiration.

Our friends and virtual company partners, Matt Starcevich and Steve Stowell, who have given so willingly of their time, ideas, and advice.

Jim and Loretta Weirauch and Chris Roessler, for their administrative, technical, and moral support.

The professional writers and journalists at business publications like *Fortune, Business Week, INC*, and the *Wall Street Journal*, whose work has fueled our passion.

The folks at Nestle. Without their support, this book would have a very different title.

And, to our families, who have been there through every single minute of this journey, we say "thank you."

# INTRODUCTION

## HOW DO THE BEST GET BETTER?

*Indeed, the chief reason for our failure in world-class competition is our failure to tap our work force's potential.*[1]

—Tom Peters

What is it that permits one organization to achieve unprecedented levels of success over a substantial period of time, while a nearly identical competitor is struggling or going down the tube? Is success the result of better mousetraps, dumb luck, or maybe just better execution? Consider, for example:

• How could Southwest Airlines achieve 23 consecutive years of record revenues and sustained profitability while TWA, Continental, Pan Am, Eastern, Braniff and others all around them were hemorrhaging red ink and going broke for the first (and maybe even second) time?

• How can GE, at a plant near Columbia, Tennessee, produce refrigerator compressors at a cost which is 20 percent less than that of its foreign competitors, despite an unfavorable labor cost differential of $15 per hour?

• In an industry long given up for dead with its heavily unionized workforces and draconian work rules—how can the Union Pacific and Burlington Northern/Santa Fe Railroads be undergoing a remarkable resurgence, with dramatically improving levels of customer service and profitability?

• Finally, will somebody please explain how, in an industry long dominated by foreign (notably Pacific Rim) competitors, Ohio-based Worthington Steel can produce steel with a quality level far in excess of the industry average, and, relative to sales, is able to outearn its Pac Rim competitors by a wide margin?

In each of the aforementioned cases, and in every other success story we have been able to find, there are some strikingly similar approaches being taken. Our mission is to discover, chronicle, and help others replicate some of those approaches. As Thomas Edison said, "There is a better way. ... Find it!"

## FATTENING THE CALVES

For approximately 30 years following the end of World War II, American companies and their workers enjoyed something of a "bubble of prosperity." Relatively unscathed compared to Europe and Japan, we were the lone industrial powerhouse left standing in the world. As a result, nations around the globe became captive markets for American goods and services (not that they weren't already clamoring for them). We enjoyed a fat and happy existence, counting the riches that came from having a monopoly on the supply side of the trade equation. Millions entered the workforce, dutifully accepted raises every six months, watched their health care and other "bennies" get better and cheaper, and the workweek get shorter. Amidst what Federal Reserve Board Chairman Alan Greenspan would have termed "irrational exuberance," millions of people allowed themselves to believe that our newfound affluence was a God-given right. *Risk* was a vanishing four-letter word, and, with the rest of the world seemingly down for the count, things like quality and productivity were deemed irrelevant.

**POOF!** The bubble burst as America awakened from its collective dream to discover that not only was the race not over, but we were on pace to finish well back in the pack. As managers across the land desperately began to reassert themselves, the blaming, rationalizing, and over-reliance on silver-bullet solutions commenced. Much was written and said at the time about the demise of commercial enterprise in the United States, that:

- we were being outdistanced by foreign competitors who took advantage of an uneven playing field,
- greed and corruption had created dangerous and destructive economic forces,

- the "New Age" workforce couldn't read, and wouldn't work,
- the blame for our economic woes rested squarely on the shoulders of a misguided, ineffectual government,
- we couldn't compete because our culture was out of tune with the modern marketplace,
- maybe we just lacked the will to succeed.

Depending on one's perspective, all or none of this may have seemed true. True or not, all that really mattered was that, in many markets and in many respects, we *were* being outperformed by others. No ifs, ands, or buts about it. All anyone had to do to find evidence (if further proof was really needed) was look at our national trade deficit; or note the change in market share of foreign vs. domestically produced products for just about any item imaginable; or compare rates of productivity growth and standard of living in the U.S. with any of a host of countries; or just listen for Ross Perot's "giant sucking sound." It wasn't and, in some cases, still isn't a pretty sight.

Obviously, though, a lot has occurred over the intervening period as many businesses in the U.S. have undergone radical and revolutionary change. Change, sometimes painful, gut-wrenching change, accompanied by more than a little confusion. Businesses by the hundreds have merged and de-merged, restructured and re-engineered, downsized and rightsized, teamed and empowered, outsourced and co-sourced. Frenetic though this activity was (and still is), it has resulted in good, substantive changes being made to the way American companies do business.

But should we mourn the death of the "good ole days?" Days when the pressure wasn't as great as it is today? When jobs were secure? When paychecks were fattened at regular intervals with scarcely any regard for worth or performance? When employees did what they were told out of fear, and the "Big Mother" corporation did everyone's worrying for them? For those who might say "yes," we've got a little advice:

**GET A GRIP!** Stop and think for a moment, and you'll realize that the good-ole days really weren't so terrific after all. Was it fun having someone else do all your thinking for you? Or, did you really enjoy having to think and take responsibility for other adult human beings? Remember what it felt like to do a job that was too narrowly defined to begin with, and then get micro-managed on top of it? How about being constantly second-guessed by legions of staff specialists in the cheap seats? How comfortable were you knowing that no matter how good a job you did, your performance and pay were going to be looked at pretty much the same way as that of everyone else? Did you like having one or two drones—co-workers (we wouldn't think of calling them peers) whose last productive act occurred too long ago to even be remembered—taking up space (and precious oxygen) in your workgroup? We didn't think so.

## BUZZWORDS ARE THE PROBLEM, NOT THE SOLUTION

Over the last two decades, there has been no shortage of quick-fix, silver-bullet solutions and how-to scenarios. We suspect that much of any benefit wrought by "vogue-word" management theories has come as the result of their forcing companies to inadvertently trip over some ugly truths about the neglected state things were in—realizations we likely would not have come to any other way.

Yet, despite the billions we've spent launching one well-intentioned managerial fad (for example, PIP, QWL, Participative Management, Teaming, Empowerment, etc.) after another, not much has changed about human nature since Elton Mayo's first studies of the relationship between motivation and productivity at the Hawthorne Works of the Western Electric Company in the late '20s. That was nearly 80 years ago! Before anyone but his mother had ever *heard* of quality guru/curmudgeon Dr. W. Edwards Deming; before the word Toyota had ever been uttered in the Western Hemisphere; and before Tom Peters, author of mega-bestselling management classics like *In Search of Excellence* and *Thriving on Chaos,* was even born!

## DISCRETIONARY EFFORT - SPEEDBRAKE OR AFTERBURNER

In a series of motivational experiments entitled the Harvard Studies, Mayo, using a real company, real managers, and real employees, first uncovered the unmistakable relationship between worker attitudes and production, or output. Essentially, Mayo learned two things:

1. That human beings are uniquely capable of regulating their involvement in and commitment to a given task or endeavor.
2. That the extent to which we do or do not fully contribute is governed more by *attitude* than by necessity, fear, or economic influence.

In a nutshell, what he learned (and what has been reinforced by a number of subsequent experiments) is that there is an increment of human effort which can be applied exclusively at the discretion of the individual. This finding led to the coining of the term "Discretionary Effort" (DE), which is defined as the difference between that level of effort which is minimally necessary, and that of which we are in fact capable. It represents the difference between obedience and high performance, and between those who are *managed* versus those who are *led*. Its expenditure is completely a matter of choice.

PERSONAL CAPABILITY
— MINIMUM REQUIREMENTS
= DISCRETIONARY EFFORT

The context within which Mayo discovered DE at Western Electric was one in which employees were, for a variety of reasons, withholding it. They were performing only at a minimally satisfactory level or, as some might put it, they kept coming to work (and getting paid) even though, for all intents and purposes, they were on strike.

The only difference between then and now is that back then, because of a fairly jobless economy and the absence of protective empowerment (the result of union-sponsored legislation), the withholding of discretionary effort was practiced in a much more covert manner. However, shortly after the conclusion of Mayo's studies, organized labor emerged as an economic force, and their weapon of choice was collective bargaining power. Its commercial implications confirmed Mayo's discovery and brought discretionary effort "out of the closet."

## IT'S YOUR PEOPLE, STUPID

As Richard Pascale of the Stanford Graduate School of Business put it, "The trouble is, 99 percent of managerial attention today is devoted to the techniques that squeeze more out of the existing paradigm—and it's killing us. Tools, techniques, and how-to recipes won't do the job without a higher order ... concept of management."[2]

As managers career wildly from one tactic (e.g., customer satisfaction) to another (e.g., re-engineering), many forget that the critical difference between a brilliant strategy and one that gets successfully executed resides in the hearts and minds of people ... your workforce. We can scream, exhort, and rattle the saber all we want, but successful organizational change cannot come about without willing participation.

In many cases, putting alternative precepts into *practice* flies dead in the face of a definition of the managerial role that's been held and nurtured for literally hundreds of years, namely the old, authoritarian, plantation-mentality scenario which features the manager as order giver, and the employee as order taker. This failure to change our outlook toward the management of human effort has, for many, become the chief impediment to competitiveness, here and elsewhere. We certainly don't lack the brains, ability, or technology.

Rather, it's a matter of *will*; specifically, the will to change. Some have it, and some haven't gotten there yet.

Our purpose is to incent those in the latter category by calling attention to a few organizations that *do* "get it," and the very real, hard, bottom line impact they (and their shareholders) are enjoying as a result.

## SUMMARY

1.  Buzzwords are the problem, not the solution. Those organizations which have enjoyed the greatest and most lasting commercial success in our society owe that success not to vogue-word management theories, but to something else.

2.  People make the difference, period. Each of us has direct and unilateral control over the amount of discretionary effort we choose to make available to the organization.

    > PERSONAL CAPABILITY
    > − MINIMUM REQUIREMENTS
    > ─────────────────────────
    > = DISCRETIONARY EFFORT

3.  Tools, techniques, and how-to recipes won't do the job without a higher order concept of management. Some things, like the good-ole days and plantation-mentality management, belong in our rear-view mirror.

# SECTION ONE

## THE PREMISE

# JUST THE FACTS

*Everyone is entitled to his own set of opinions, but no one is entitled to his own set of facts.*

—James Schlesinger

## THE XYZ 500: IT'S LIKE A BROKEN RECORD AT THE TOP OF THE CHARTS

Every year, respected business publications like *Fortune, INC,* and *Business Week* rank those companies that are doing the best job in their chosen industry or market. We read about the Most Admired and Best Managed, those generating the Highest Shareholder Return, Greatest Market Value, the XYZ 500; and the list goes on.

Caught in this annual downpour of rankings and ratings, we can't help but notice that with almost monotonous regularity the organizations nailing down these honors are the same ones, year after year. You know the names: Coca Cola, Merck, GE, Southwest Airlines, Intel, Nordstrom, 3M, USAA, Johnson & Johnson, and Hewlett-Packard, to list only a few.

Outside the corporate boardroom, but no less engaged in the world of business, lies the arena of professional sports. Here, too, the same teams perennially rise to the top—dynasties like the San Francisco 49ers, Los Angeles Dodgers, and Chicago Bulls.

Since 1982, *Fortune* has published an annual listing of the "Most Admired Corporations," ranking—overall and by industry— those organizations with the best business reputations. Approximately 11,000 corporate executives, outside directors, and financial analysts judge companies according to the following criteria:

- quality of management
- quality of products and services
- value as a long-term investment
- use of corporate assets
- financial soundness
- innovativeness
- community and environmental responsibility
- ability to attract, develop, and keep talented people

In the 1996 version of this report, *Fortune's* Anne B. Fisher noted a thread running through the list when she wrote that "12 of the top 15 have great brands."[1] Likewise, she would have been correct had she observed that *all* of those same top 15 companies also happen to be regarded as exceptional places to work. In fact, nine of them have at one time or another been included in the *100 Best Companies to Work for in America*.[2] Similarly, *none* of the "100 Best" companies shows up in (or anywhere near) the bottom 50 on *Fortune's* list.

| COMPANY | MOST ADMIRED RANK | SCORE | "100 BEST" |
|---------|-------------------|-------|------------|
| COCA COLA | 1 | 8.70 | — |
| PROCTER & GAMBLE | 2 | 8.55 | YES |
| RUBBERMAID | 3 | 8.35 | — |
| JOHNSON & JOHNSON | 4 | 8.32 | YES |
| INTEL | 5 | 8.30 | YES |
| MERCK | 6 | 8.26 | YES |
| MICROSOFT | 7 (TIE) | 8.23 | YES |
| MIRAGE RESORTS | 7 (TIE) | 8.23 | — |
| HEWLETT-PACKARD | 9 (TIE) | 8.19 | YES |
| MOTOROLA | 9 (TIE) | 8.19 | YES |
| 3M | 11 | 8.08 | YES |
| PFIZER | 12 | 8.06 | — |
| DISNEY | 13 (TIE) | 8.05 | YES |
| MCDONALDS | 13 (TIE) | 8.05 | — |
| GILLETTE | 15 | 8.00 | — |

In similar fashion, and on the premise that organizations are best known by their competitors, *Fortune* asked executives to rate companies in their own industries on measures like quality of management, financial soundness, and innovation. Here again, the results could hardly be more compelling. In case after case, the best places to work showed up at or near the top of industry rankings.[3] Some examples:

| INDUSTRY | COMPANY | RANK | "100 BEST" |
|---|---|---|---|
| COMPUTERS & OFFICE EQUIP. | HEWLETT-PACKARD | 1 | YES |
| AIRLINES | SOUTHWEST | 1 | YES |
| PACKAGE & FREIGHT DELIVERY | FEDEX | 2 | YES |
| ELECTRONICS | GE | 3 | YES |
| SCIENTIFIC, PHOTO, CONTROL EQUIPMENT | 3M | 1 | YES |
| COMPUTER & DATA SERVICES | MICROSOFT | 1 | YES |
| PUBLISHING & PRINTING | R.R. DONNELLEY | 2 | YES |
| ENTERTAINMENT | DISNEY | 1 | YES |
| PHARMACEUTICALS | JOHNSON & JOHNSON | 1 | YES |
| PHARMACEUTICALS | MERCK | 2 | YES |
| CHEMICALS | DUPONT | 1 | YES |
| BUILDING MATERIALS | CORNING | 1 | YES |
| SOAPS & COSMETICS | PROCTER & GAMBLE | 1 | YES |
| GENERAL MERCHANDISE | WAL-MART | 1 | YES |
| GENERAL MERCHANDISE | NORDSTROM | 2 | YES |
| GENERAL MERCHANDISE | J. C. PENNEY | 3 | YES |
| APPAREL | LEVI STRAUSS | 1 | YES |
| FURNITURE | HERMAN MILLER | 2 | YES |
| METALS | NUCOR | 2 | YES |

For those who require a little harder financial evidence, the same publication, in December 1996, published an article based on Stern Stewart & Company's ranking of 1,000 corporations. Utilizing what many consider to be the two most effective measures of financial performance, Stern Stewart rated the corporations by Market Value Added (MVA), and Economic Value Added (EVA).[4] As its name implies, MVA describes the extent to which a company's stock has, over its lifetime, either enriched or impoverished investors. It shows the difference between what they have put in and what they can take out. EVA, on the other hand, represents a company's after-tax net operating profit minus its cost of capital (both debt and equity).

In this case, eight of the top 10 companies rated on MVA also appear among the *100 Best Companies to Work for in America*. Five corporations (Coca Cola, Johnson & Johnson, Merck, Microsoft, and Procter & Gamble) made the top 10 on *both* the "Most Admired" and "Highest MVA" lists, and four of those five also happen to be "100 Best" companies.

| COMPANY | MOST ADMIRED RANK (SCALE = 1–417) | MVA RANK (SCALE = 1–1,000) | "100 BEST" |
|---|---|---|---|
| COCA COLA | 1 | 1 | — |
| MERCK | 6 | 3 | YES |
| MICROSOFT | 7 | 5 | YES |
| JOHNSON & JOHNSON | 4 | 6 | YES |
| PROCTER & GAMBLE | 2 | 8 | YES |

At the opposite end of the spectrum, some organizations with not so stellar reputations as employers wind up near the bottom of the "Most Admired" or MVA/EVA rankings, or both. In many respects they are neither winning organizations, nor are they perceived as especially great places to work.

| COMPANY | MOST ADMIRED RANK (SCALE = 1–417) | MVA RANK (SCALE = 1–1,000) |
|---|---|---|
| KMART | 415 | 996 |
| GENERAL MOTORS | 288 | 998 |
| US AIRWAYS | 414 | 538 |
| TWA | 417 | — |

## WHERE'S THE BEEF?

So what's the point? Actually, it's a simple one. So simple, in fact, that Carnation Company may have put it best many years ago when they suggested that their condensed milk product came "From Contented Cows."[5]

Any dairy farmer will tell you that for as long as cows have been milked, methods of care have been employed to produce healthier, more contented, and, most importantly, higher-yielding cows. In a similar vein, those organizations that can be consistently identified as winners in their respective fields, whether it's making jet aircraft engines or pharmaceuticals, delivering urgent packages, writing auto insurance policies, or merely "playing games," also happen to be known as some of the best places on earth to work. Unlike the age-old conundrum of the chicken and the egg, in this case we don't think there is any doubt about which came first.

From the start, the exceptional organizations have differentiated themselves as employers of choice, thus enabling them to hire and retain top-drawer people, and *then* differentiated their products and services in the marketplace. Think it's a coincidence? We don't.

We have a lot to say about what *Contented Cow* companies are doing, but perhaps just as notable is what they *aren't* doing. Unlike the approach being taken by many of their competitors, the management of these companies is not betting the ranch that technology and capital spending alone will lead them to a more competitive posture. But don't confuse contentment with complacency. The fact that a cow is contented in no way interferes with its inclination or ability to "jump over the moon." Instead, companies that follow the *Contented Cow* path seem to be in agreement with the idea, beautifully expressed by Owen (Brad) Butler, former chairman and CEO of Procter & Gamble, that "productivity comes from people, not machines."

> *From the start, the truly excellent organizations have differentiated themselves as employers of choice.*

It has been said that "the only way for any organization to ensure its financial security is by creating satisfied, loyal customers."[6] To the extent that the organization is at all labor-dependent, we propose that the principal requirement for operationalizing that aim is the creation of a satisfied, fully engaged workforce. In the main, our products and services, technology, methods, tools, and strategies can *all* be copied. But it's not as easy to duplicate a focused, caring workforce. In the final analysis, "people factors" are frequently *the* key source of competitive advantage—the factor least visible to the naked eye and most difficult to emulate. Sooner or later, we must come to grips with the fact that most businesses aren't so much capital- or expertise- or even product-driven as they are PEOPLE-driven.

That hasn't always been the case. Under the earliest business model, the corporation was little more than a tangible piece of property—at first a piece of real estate (for example, a farm), and later a factory. Then over time it became the financiers, those who had supplied the capital necessary to expand and automate the farm or factory, who emerged as the primary centers of influence. But as the very nature of work continues to evolve, and its focus shifts more to knowledge, service, and speed, the significance of the hard assets and those who technically own them diminishes. From now on, corporations will be defined less by their tangible presence and more by the real pulsating bodies who comprise them—customers, employees, and owners.

> *Take away my factories, and I will build a new and better factory; but take away my people, and grass will grow on the factory floor.*
> —Andrew Carnegie

## JUST THE FACTS

To determine if there was any factual basis to our premise about *Contented Cows* and better milk, we first set out to identify a group of companies which are widely recognized as being employers of choice. We weren't interested in identifying those outfits that have somehow managed to garner a good reputation quickly. Rather, we focused on the ones that have done it the hard way—over at least a 10-year period—and have managed to keep their reputations intact through good times and bad. Nobody ever drowned in honest sweat.

We relied on three main sources to separate the *Contented Cows* from the rest of the herd:

1.  The book, *100 Best Companies to Work For in America*
    (1984, 1985 and 1993 editions). Four of the six
    *Contented Cow* companies made the '84 list, and five
    of them made it in '85 and again in '93, with Southwest
    finally included in the most recent version. (In our view,
    they should have been there sooner. It's one of the few
    late arrivals anybody has seen from Southwest.)
2.  Our colleagues in the Society for Human Resource
    Management, who have been consulted extensively
    on the subject.
3.  Our own judgment based on 20-plus years of business
    experience. In the final analysis, we asked ourselves this
    question: "Is this a company that we would be proud
    and pleased to work for?"

Our task was made more difficult by the fact that we felt it
important to identify organizations that were fairly representative of the broad spectrum of commerce. We included some from
heavy manufacturing, some from the service sector, some from
the world of high tech, some from retail, etc. You get the picture.
While we ultimately settled on six organizations as the *Contented
Cow* representatives, a handful of others easily could have qualified, including some strong personal favorites like Johnson &
Johnson, Disney, Citicorp, Marriott, and Intel.

After the *Contented Cows* were identified, our focus then
shifted to the task of finding comparable organizations, or *Common Cows*, against which to benchmark them. We first identified
organizations in the same basic business or industry. Then, we
searched for companies that compete in a significant way with the
the six *Contented Cows*, and that most people would recognize.
Size was not an issue. Nor did we attempt to bias the research by
culling and keeping acorn calves (mismatched weaklings), against
which to run the exemplars. It would have been quite easy, for
example, to pit the U.S. Postal Service against FedEx; or TWA, or
the now defunct Eastern Airlines against Southwest. (It was hard
to resist the temptation, but somehow we managed.)

Our purpose is not (repeat, NOT) to bash one set of companies or to hold the *Contented Cow* group out as models of perfection, because they aren't. It *is* an attempt to validate something that we feel has for too long existed only as a sentimental notion on the part of many. We hope to alter this misperception and illuminate, from a somewhat different perspective, some of the distinct and valuable advantages of effective employee relations practices.

We've identified the 12 *Contented Cow* and *Common Cow* companies for the aforementioned reasons. But we didn't limit our research to these comparison organizations. Throughout the following chapters, we'll give examples gleaned from both personal experiences and interviews with people from many other organizations, some of which will no doubt be familiar to you. However, in all of our analysis, the test for being considered a *Contented Cow* company required that the organization meet the following minimum criteria:

1. **Profitability** – a consistent track record of growth in revenue and earnings.
2. **Continuity** – in business for at least five years (except in industries younger than five years, as in the case of Netscape, and a few other high tech firms.)
3. **Desirability** – be generally regarded by the people who work there as good places to work, with positive, affirming, sensible, and affordable employee relations practices.

## THE FINE PRINT

From the start, we readily admit that real (and lasting) success in business requires more than just enlightened employee relations practices. You must have market-worthy products or services, the ability to deliver them when and where the customer wants at a price they're willing to pay, and, to be sure, capable leadership.

We also recognize that just as productive employees are not always satisfied, satisfied employees are not always productive.

In fact, some may be satisfied because they don't *have* to be productive. And, of course, there are those who prefer to "check their brains" at the door and work only with their bodies (if at all).

So, we are not asking you to accept the notion that the ONLY factor explaining the huge financial performance advantage of the *Contented Cow* companies happens to be their employment practices. But, we *are* asking you to consider the possibility that

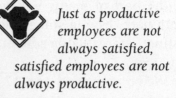

*Just as productive employees are not always satisfied, satisfied employees are not always productive.*

it's impossible for any labor-intensive business to get to (let alone stay at) the top *without* having adopted such practices. We think the facts and figures you're about to see make the case in no uncertain terms. You be the judge.

In the course of our research, we pored over 10 years' worth of financials for dozens of companies. For comparison purposes, we settled on the 10-year period from 1986 to 1995, and on financial measures that were statistically significant, universally available, and commonly understood. Having established the background and parameters, here is our list of comparison companies:

| CONTENTED COWS | COMMON COWS |
| --- | --- |
| HEWLETT-PACKARD(HWP) | TEXAS INSTRUMENTS (TXN) |
| FEDEX (FDX) | CONSOLIDATED FREIGHTWAYS (CNF) |
| GENERAL ELECTRIC (GE) | GENERAL MOTORS (GM) |
| SOUTHWEST AIRLINES (LUV) | UNITED AIRLINES (UAL) |
| WAL-MART (WMT) | SEARS (S) |
| 3M (MMM) | XEROX (XRX) |

*Has anyone ever sung the glory of the cow?*[7]

—Frank Lloyd Wright

Now, before going any further, ask yourself this question: "Based on what I know of these companies, which of them would I go to work for?" In fact, while you're at it, why not make a list of your own comparison companies? That way, if you at all doubt our premise, you can check their financials and see for yourself. Go ahead, it's okay to write in the book—you paid for it.

> The Contented Cows outgrew the Common Cows by a margin of roughly four to one.

My list of Comparison Companies:

**CONTENTED**                          **COMMON**

1. _____                 _____

2. _____                 _____

3. _____                 _____

4. _____                 _____

5. _____                 _____

## SIGNIFICANT OBSERVATIONS:

1. As shown in the following table, and again in Figure 1.1, at the beginning of the measurement period (1986), the *Common Cow* companies were, in aggregate, nearly three times the size of their *Contented Cow* counterparts, measured in annual revenues.

| CONTENTED COWS | '86 REV. (MILL) | COMMON COWS | '86 REV. (MILL) |
|---|---|---|---|
| GE | 36,782 | GM | 102,814 |
| LUV | 769 | UAL | 7,119 |
| MMM | 8,602 | XRX | 9,781 |
| FDX | 2,573 | CNF | 2,124 |
| HWP | 7,102 | TXN | 4,974 |
| WMT | 8,451 | S | 44,282 |
| TOTAL | 64,279 | TOTAL | 171,094 |
| AVG. | 10,713 | AVG. | 28,516 |

*Source:* Moody's

**FIGURE 1.1**

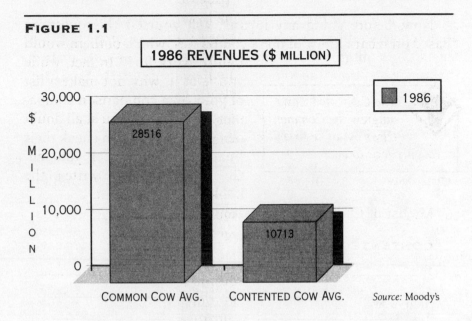

1986 REVENUES ($ MILLION)

2. Over the ensuing 10-year comparison period (1986–1995), the initial revenue gap was closed significantly as the *Contented Cows* outgrew the *Common Cows* by a margin of roughly four to one. (See Figure 1.2)

**FIGURE 1.2**

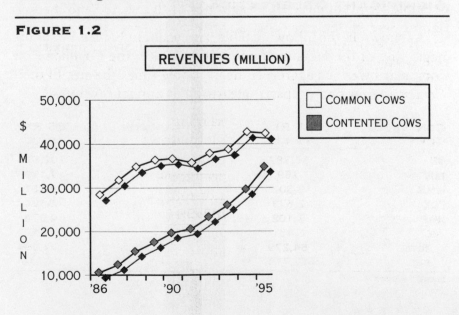

REVENUES (MILLION)

3. Performance in the sales growth area is not simply a matter of "averages beating averages." In *five out of six cases*, the *Contented Cows* outgrew the *Common Cows* by a substantial margin; the lone exception was Xerox, which nudged out 3M by a hair.

## 10 YEAR SALES GROWTH

| COMPANY | % GROWTH | COMPANY | % GROWTH |
|---------|----------|---------|----------|
| GE | 90.39% | GM | 64.21% |
| LUV | 273.60% | UAL | 109.90% |
| MMM | 56.48% | XRX | 69.83% |
| FDX | 265.02% | CNF | 148.63% |
| HWP | 343.80% | TXN | 163.93% |
| WMT | 876.14% | S | -21.13% |
| AVG. | 317.57% | AVG. | 89.23% |
| WEIGHTED AVG. | 226.34% | WEIGHTED AVG. | 48.29% |

Source: Moody's

4. On the premise that companies in the same line of business should be somewhat comparable in their degree of labor dependence and the skill mix required of their workers, AND that, all things being equal, they would enjoy relatively the same levels of employee productivity, we examined both revenue and income figures on a per-employee basis.

As shown in figure 1.3, the 10-year sales growth comparison is every bit as stark when cast in this fashion.

**FIGURE 1.3**

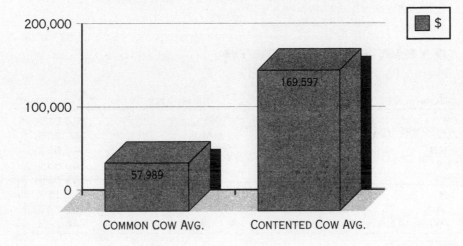

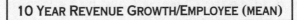

*Contented people give better performances.*[8]

—Tommy Lasorda

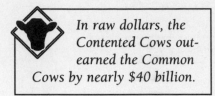

*In raw dollars, the Contented Cows out-earned the Common Cows by nearly $40 billion.*

5. Performance of the *Contented Cows* relative to their *Common* counterparts on the profit front is equally as compelling, if not more so. As shown in Figure 1.4, net income of the *Contented Cows* grew by 202 percent over the 10-year period, versus 139 percent for the *Common Cows*.

**FIGURE 1.4**

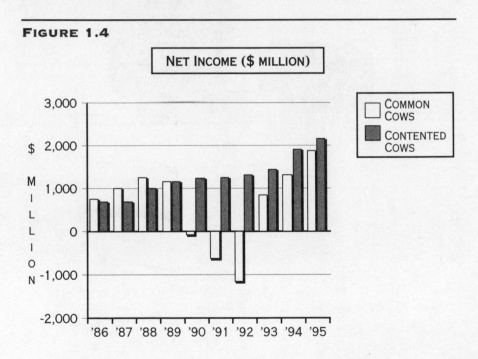

NET INCOME ($ MILLION)

6. Of much greater significance is the fact that, in raw dollars, the *Contented Cows* outearned the *Common Cows* by nearly $40 billion over the 10-year period. Earnings of the average *Contented Cow* company were roughly double those of their *Common* counterparts. (See Figure 1.5)

| COMPANY | 10 YR. NET INCOME ($ MILLION) | COMPANY | 10 YR. NET INCOME ($ MILLION) |
|---|---|---|---|
| GE | 42,071 | GM | 21,035 |
| LUV | 881 | UAL | 576 |
| MMM | 11,351 | XRX | 4,780 |
| FDX | 1,334 | CNF | 382 |
| HWP | 10,057 | TXN | 3,046 |
| WMT | 13,226 | S | 9,841 |
| TOTAL | 78,920 | TOTAL | 39,660 |
| AVG. | 13,153 | AVG. | 6,610 |

Source: Moody's

**FIGURE 1.5**

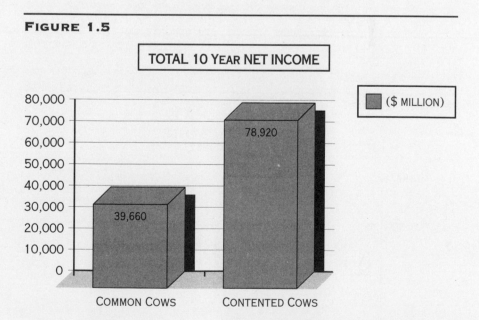

TOTAL 10 YEAR NET INCOME

7. On a per-employee basis, as shown in Figure 1.6A and B, the *Contented Cows* again substantially outperformed their counterparts.

**FIGURE 1.6A**

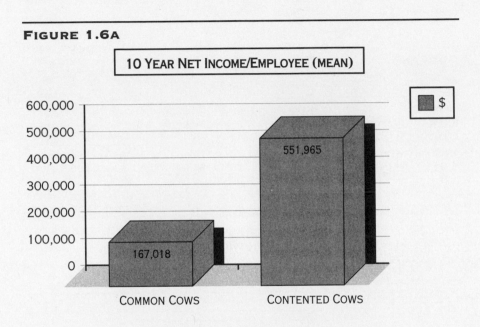

**10 YEAR NET INCOME/EMPLOYEE (MEAN)**

**FIGURE 1.6B**

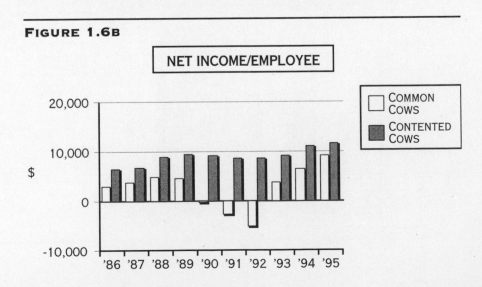

**NET INCOME/EMPLOYEE**

Here again, it's not just a matter of averages. In all six cases, the *Contented Cows* positively outmilked their competitors when it came to net income per employee, outearning them by a factor of three.

| COMPANY | 10 YEAR NET INC. PER EMPL. (MEAN) | COMPANY | 10 YEAR NET INC. PER EMPL. (MEAN) |
|---------|-----------------------------------|---------|-----------------------------------|
| GE  | 151,662 | GM  | 27,881 |
| LUV | 82,144  | UAL | 7,788  |
| MMM | 134,471 | XRX | 47,824 |
| FDX | 18,225  | CNF | 12,431 |
| HWP | 109,733 | TXN | 45,221 |
| WMT | 41,267  | S   | 24,708 |

The "net income per employee" case is even more impressive when one considers the fact that over the 10-year period, the *Contented Cow* companies generated an average of 79,000 new jobs per company while the *Common Cows lost* on average 61,000! .

**FIGURE 1.7**

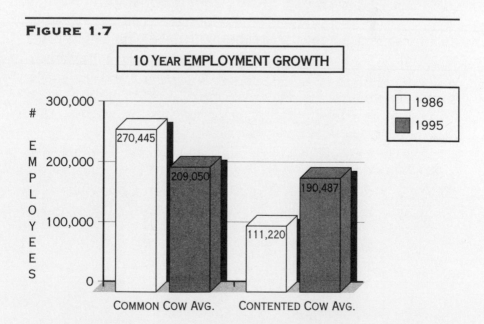

## A "HEAD-TO-HEAD" COMPARISON

Perhaps nowhere are the comparisons more stark than in the transportation sector. Carrying both human cargo and packages, four of the 12 companies do business in that sector, competing on a head-to-head basis.

Some might argue that the Federal Express vs. Consolidated Freight comparison is unfair because FedEx operates predominantly in the high priority end of the market. Yet, consider the fact that Emery Worldwide (owned by CF since 1989) not only was in that business, but dominated it before FedEx founder and CEO Fred Smith ever went to business school! So what was it that propelled FedEx to an average annual sales growth of 26 percent compared to CF's 14.9 percent and provided a net income per employee of $18,225 to CF's $12,431?

> *In all six cases, the Contented Cows positively outmilked their competitors when it came to Net Income per Employee, outearning them by a factor of three.*

Southwest Airlines provides yet another clear-cut example. Relative to their competitors (not just United), they have fewer total employees per aircraft (79 versus 131); carry more passengers per employee (2,318 versus 848); have more available "seat miles" per employee (1,891,082 versus 1,339,995); enjoy a better reputation with their customers; and oh, by the way, they make more money.

How? In view of the fact that the regulations and capital costs under which each operates are nearly identical—planes are planes, trucks are trucks, fares are fares, routes are routes—the whole milking match pretty well comes down to whether or not "my people can outshoot and out-move yours."

## MOVE IT OR LOSE IT

Consider the case of now defunct Eastern Airlines. Throughout most of its history as a commercial airline, Eastern competed on a head-to-head basis with Delta Air Lines. At one time during the competitive struggle between the two air carriers, the overlap of the markets they served approached 70 percent. Despite flying the same type aircraft (primarily mid-size Boeings and DC-9s) to the same cities, charging the same fares, and serving the same lousy food, one company died a very slow, painful death, and the other survived. What made the difference?

*The whole milking match pretty well comes down to whether or not "my people can outshoot and out-move yours."*

Well, in the case of Delta, their people were free to focus on attending to nothing but *customer* needs, secure in the knowledge that they were going to be treated fairly and respectfully by the company and their managers. In 1981, a fully engaged Delta workforce decided to chip in and buy the company a little present—a Boeing 767 jet! Conversely, at Eastern, employees were so balled-up worrying about their own work-related problems that they had precious little time, energy, or inclination to attend to the needs of paying customers.

## THE SKYJACKED LUNCH

Noted author and consultant Charles Garfield tells a story which makes the point crystal clear. It seems that Garfield was on a lengthy, four-hour Eastern flight one day when a flight attendant approached his first class seat during the meal service with the news that she had run out of entrees—not just his preferred entree, but *all* of them. Despite having been hungry even before boarding the plane, and the fact that his nearest food was now several more hours away, Garfield decided to make the best of a bad situation by immersing himself in his work. His seatmate, on the other hand, apparently went "postal" over the matter, berating the airline, the flight attendants, and making all the usual threats.

After a while, Garfield got up to stretch and visit the restroom. On the way, he passed the galley, which had the curtains drawn around it. Deciding to stop and offer the flight attendants some consolation over his neighbor's rudeness, Garfield drew aside the curtains and found, to his amazement, two flight attendants consuming his and his seatmate's meals! At which point, one of them remarked, "Well, we've got to eat too, you know."[9]

## THEY LOVE TO SMILE AND IT SHOWS

Around that same time, I* made a trip from Memphis to Salt Lake City on Delta. In Dallas, I boarded a packed 727 along with about 130 other souls. There was not an empty seat. With temperatures approaching 100 degrees, we sat on the plane for over an hour due to air traffic control delays. During that time, many passengers missed their connecting flights in Salt Lake City. We were not what you would call a happy bunch of people.

Midway into the flight, I was struck by the fact that, despite physical discomfort and personal inconvenience, the whole tenor of the people on the plane had changed from one of extreme agitation to a pleasant calm. Knowing they hadn't rolled a free booze cart down the aisle, I couldn't figure out what had caused the change. Then at one point during the meal service, I looked up and there stood all three flight attendants poised over passengers with meal trays—SMILING! These three women had accomplished with smiles what a fistful of free drink coupons and a rash of apologies could have *never* done.

Returning from the same trip a few days later, my flight was one of the last passenger flights to arrive that evening; the airline counters were all closed and the airport was deserted. I realized that I was well short of the amount of cash required to

---

* Authors' Note: Assuming the reader to be indifferent when it comes to the details of our personal lives, we have refrained from inserting ourselves into the narrative by not attributing anecdotes to either one of us. It suffices to say that no matter whose story it may be, we both agree on the lesson drawn from it.

retrieve my car from the parking garage. (They didn't accept credit cards, and my ATM card was elsewhere.) On the way to baggage claim, I happened into a fellow in a Delta uniform, a counter agent by the name of Boyd Collins. I introduced myself, told him about my problem, and asked if there was any way he could help me get a check cashed. Boyd explained that since the Delta counter was closed, and the cash had been locked up for the evening, his company couldn't do much for me. My heart sank momentarily. Then, without hesitation, he reached for his wallet, pulled out $50 of his own money, and said he'd be happy to cash my check.

Now some may argue that these two situations were highly unusual. Garfield happened to be on a flight with a couple of flight attendants who, for one reason or another, were just having a bad day, while I simply got lucky and stumbled into the equivalent of Santa Claus. Don't believe it. Anyone who has flown enough to know the difference between an aisle and a center seat knows better. The acts of these employees were *fully* representative of their respective organizations at the time.*

## THE CORE OF OUR PHILOSOPHY

Before going further, let's get something straight. Our message concerning enlightened employee relations has nothing whatsoever to do with social or humanitarian interests. Instead, it's all about capitalism, pure and simple.

Or as Jim Barksdale, former chief operating officer of Federal Express and the current CEO of

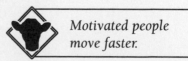
*Motivated people move faster.*

---

*It's ironic perhaps that Delta has of late flirted with some of the same destructive behavior that led to the undoing of first Eastern and later Texas Air. Caught in a vise created by a rapidly changing air transport market and the need to reduce operating expenses, the company has seemingly lost its way. In the process, a once proud workforce has grown increasingly dispirited and confused as the company's long standing "no furlough covenant" has been shaken, if not shattered, and the organization struggles with its identity. Do they want to be a no frills discount carrier a-la ValuJet, or a "real" airline? To some degree admitting the problem, then CEO Ron Allen said, "In some cases, we did cut too deeply." See *Business Week* (1/20/97), p. 30. Let's hope they get it figured out before they too pay the price.

Netscape, put it when describing the underlying rationale for the people philosophy at FedEx, "Motivated people move faster. Our people philosophy is not out of a spirit of altruism. You have fewer problems and make more money."[10] Charles Hampden-Turner of the London Business School puts it another way: "It's not just wrong to exploit workers, it's stupid. ... The trouble with crushing workers is that then you have to try to make high quality products with crushed people."

We'll say it again. What we are advocating is not the advancement of any social or humanitarian cause, but capitalism at its very best. Are the concepts of satisfied people and capitalism mutually exclusive? Of course not! In fact, they are inextricably linked.

> *Our message concerning enlightened employee relations has nothing whatsoever to do with social or humanitarian interests.*

There are those, however, who report to work each morning reciting a mantra which goes a little like this: "We're here for one reason and one reason only—to enhance shareholder wealth," and that's okay. But in our view, a problem emerges when that laudable goal is allowed to become the narrow, or even exclusive, focus of attention. To wit, the organization may actually be precluded from doing certain things, which in the long run, would otherwise best serve shareholder interests.

Levi Strauss CEO Robert Haas apparently agrees. "Everyone looks at the wrong end of the telescope, as if profits drive the business. Financial reporting doesn't get to the real stuff—employee morale, turnover, consumer satisfaction, on-time delivery, consumer attitudes, perceptions of the brand, purchase intentions—that drives financial results."[11]

## YOUR REPUTATION IS WORTH MORE THAN YOU THINK

What is your reputation as an employer worth? What sort of things should you be doing to maintain and enhance that reputation? Organizations which don't measure up tend to be viewed as an employer of last resort; nobody with any brains, ability, or motivation wants to work there! When this occurs, only two things can happen. Either the organization is forced to pay market-premium wages and salaries in an attempt to secure better applicants, or it must accept the lower quality applicants, or do both. And, while the impact of bad hiring won't show up in the earnings for this quarter or next, rest assured it *will* show up.

One *very* capitalistic organization that has taken this lesson to heart is GE. At one time GE had a somewhat less-than-sterling reputation as an employer, and the company suffered because of it. However, due in large part to Jack Welch's leadership, the company has steadily worked its way back. Having re-established its reputation as an excellent place to work, GE has become a targeted destination for some of the very best and brightest folks in business. They've managed to recruit one of the "deepest benches" anywhere in the corporate world. To those who might say "so what?" consider these questions: If GE, and others like them have talented people begging and practically fighting to go to work there, do you suppose their managers find the task of recruiting easier or harder? Do they have to pay people relatively more, or less to work there? Now contrast that with your own situation, and a 1996 Conference Board study reflecting that 43 percent of companies surveyed reported problems finding and keeping high-quality workers.

> *Organizations which don't measure up tend to be viewed as an employer of last resort; nobody with any brains, ability, or motivation wants to work there!*

## PRAGMATIC IDEALS

If we boil all this down, what remains is a set of beliefs and practices driven by a great sense of pragmatism. According to Haas, "I believe that if you create an environment that your people identify with, that is responsive to their sense of values, justice, fairness, ethics, compassion, and appreciation, they will help you be successful. There's no guarantee—but I will stake all my chips on this vision."[12] Look at what works, and emulate it.

Lands' End President and CEO Mike Smith summed it up for us in the following note:

> *The title of your book would create a few smiles and knowing nods of the head among our agricultural neighbors here in Dodgeville, Wisconsin, as well as among the majority of our Lands' End Employees. Although it's difficult to give you the bottom line in dollars and cents … I can relate some examples that may help.*
>
> *Our retention rate for hourly and salaried positions is extremely high. That creates costs savings in recruiting, hiring, and training for us. With over 3,000 employees in these positions, there is a substantial savings here.*
>
> *We have been ranked as one of the 100 Best Companies to Work For in America. Our pride in our work and friendliness received the highest ratings. This turns into recruitment savings by having a culture that people look for and that our own employees refer qualified candidates to. The effect is a top quality candidate pool combined with the previously mentioned retention which results in a great work force.*
>
> *Our employee friendliness directly affects our customers, resulting in high customer satisfaction. We receive thousands of customer letters annually that reflect how much they appreciate our quality products and our service level. This definitely has a bottom line impact …*
>
> *Sincerely,*
>
> *Mike Smith*
> *President and CEO, Lands' End*

So why not do what Lands' End, GE, Levi Strauss, and other employers of choice have done? Build an organization full of capitalists—people with pride and a critical stake in the enterprise. Try to look at the situation logically. If management wants one thing, and employees want the opposite, it's a simple high school physics problem. There's more of them than there are of you, and the side with the most mass and energy is going to prevail. For as long as this goal incongruence exists, each side is going to spend its time accumulating or withholding energy rather than being productive. In the end, everybody loses.

Faced in the '80s with the entry of UPS into the next-day priority air express market, FedEx applied this lesson in a big way. Wanting to make United Parcel's debut as painful and expensive as possible, the company contemplated "raising the bar" by changing the next-day service standard on delivery commitments from noon to 10:30 A.M. The 90-minute difference doesn't seem like much until you consider that it represented about a 40 percent reduction in the time available for sorting somewhere on the order of a million packages each night.

Time and again the company's planners and industrial engineers calculated the number of additional package handlers and sorters they would need to hire in order to pull it off, and each time it added up to a financial disaster. Finally, Hub Operations Vice President Karl Birkholz—who will likely forget more about discretionary effort and goal congruence than Elton Mayo ever knew—proposed that what they really needed to do in order to "help the python choke down this pig" was to rework "the deal" for his 3,000 or so college-aged, hourly paid, part-time employees whose job it was to sort all those packages.

> *If management wants one thing, and employees want the opposite, it's a simple high-school physics problem.*

Recognizing that the company's objective (getting the packages sorted and the planes out quicker) and his employees' objective (making more money) were fundamentally at odds, Birkholz simply proposed giving his workers a minimum weekly hours guarantee that would allow them to go home (with pay) when their work was done. The company enacted the scheme and productivity went through the roof, allowing FedEx to profitably blunt their new competitor's foray into the overnight express market.

*Care of the cow brings good fortune.*[13]

—I Ching, or Book of Changes

# CONTENTED COWS:
# A HISTORICAL PERSPECTIVE

## ROBERT OWEN AND SCOTTISH MILLWORKERS

The concept of *Contented Cows* is certainly not new. It has some impressive historical precedent both in the United States and abroad. Even in cases where the concept's application has been flawed (and there have been several), it teaches us valuable lessons.

For the first quarter of the 19th century, Robert Owen owned and operated a highly successful cotton mill at New Lanark, in southwestern Scotland. Before you get visions of kilted lads and lassies frolicking in the heather, you should know that to work in a factory during Britain's industrial revolution was no day at the loch. At the time, Scotland's industrial belt was home to poverty, backbreaking labor, and deplorable working conditions. But Owen believed that one's character was a product both of inherited nature and of one's environment. Knowing he could do nothing to affect the former, he conducted an experiment in the latter, and created for a time, one of Britain's most flourishing and profitable corporations—with a large labor force enjoying working conditions far surpassing the low standards of that era.

Owen inherited a population of just under a thousand demoralized, unproductive workers. Gradually, he turned it into a group of 2,500 industrious and—compared to most of their fellow countrypersons—relatively satisfied members of society. He accomplished this feat by creating a work climate more conducive to human effort, and then gradually enriching the pot.

While his competitors worked their people 13 to 14 hours a day, the beneficent Owen required only 10½ hours a day from the adults in the mill, and less than that from the children! (When they weren't working, they attended the schools he had built for them.) While even those hours seem draconian by today's standards, it was a groundbreaking development in early Victorian Britain.

Turnover was a problem for Owen's contemporaries. Not so much because workers quit, but because they had the annoying habit of dying, often in their thirties. Although there was not much field research on which Owen could base his hypothesis, he theorized that creating a community in which workers could live to a ripe old age and focus their energy on their work, rather than their problems, could only bring in more profits for him and his partner. His theory proved to be valid and, for more than a generation, made him a wealthy man.

The milltown, beautifully preserved today as a popular attraction on the banks of the River Clyde, near Glasgow, promised not only humane treatment of workers and more reasonable working conditions, but featured a strong emphasis on education. All employees' children, from the age of 2, were enrolled in superior schools in the village. Shopping, healthcare, and even social outlets and recreation were provided, all without leaving New Lanark.

What motivated Robert Owen? From the outset, he seemed very much a capitalist. He figured that workers distracted by trying to survive couldn't possibly produce as much for him as people who at least had a fighting chance of attending to their own basic needs. Even Frederick Engels, unabashed socialist and coauthor of the infamous *Communist Manifesto*, said that Owen's philosophy and practices were "based upon this purely business foundation, the outcome, so to say, of commercial calculation. Throughout, [his practices] maintained this practical character."[14]*

---

*In later years, Owen lost sight of the pragmatism that Engels recognized in him, became preoccupied with developing a utopian society, and screwed the whole thing up. Eventually, social idealism overtook the straightforward, practical ideology on which New Lanark was founded, and the community, along with its American counterpart, New Harmony, Indiana (also established by Owen), failed. Both communities stopped emphasizing the honor of labor, and the paternalism that evolved in its place attracted loafers and bums who liked the idea of being taken care of. See Cliff Hanley, *History of Scotland* (Gallery Books, 1986), p. 98.

## MILTON HERSHEY AND THE TOWN THAT CHOCOLATE BUILT

A century later, another pragmatist built a community, one which remains today—a community built of chocolate. Milton S. Hershey stumbled onto candy making after a series of small enterprises collapsed behind him. He literally went from rags to riches in four short years, and in the process, built the town of Hershey, Pennsylvania. Some said his success was due to his willingness to peel off his coat and work beside any of his workers any time. Others said it was the candy maker's motto, "Stick to it." Still others attributed his company's explosive and then sustained growth to Hershey's recognition that if you take care of certain basic needs for people so they can concentrate on their work, they'll make money for you. (As evidenced by Hershey's rank on Stern Stewart's MVA list—140th in 1996, with MVA of $3.4 billion—they've done quite well in this regard.)[15]

Hershey's practical approach to the business he built emanated not so much from ideology, but from necessity. When he decided to build a chocolate factory, he couldn't afford to buy land in the more developed areas of his homestate of Pennsylvania, but the price of land in the central part of the state was very attractive. There was only one problem; nobody lived out there. Undaunted, Hershey built not only a chocolate plant, but an entire town. He made housing available, put in schools, a bank, hotel (stay there if you ever have the chance), churches, parks, golf courses, and a zoo. He even installed an extensive trolley system to provide transportation for those who settled in the new town of Hershey. During the Great Depression, rather than laying off and retrenching, Hershey hired and grew.

### RUMINATE ON THIS

Look, we're not pushing any kind of idyllic society. Far from it. Times have changed, and a company's practices must reflect its operating environment. In Victorian Scotland, people needed shelter, medicine, hours that wouldn't kill them, and education for their children. And crass as it may sound, Robert Owen knew that every young widowed mother mourning the premature death of her husband represented another fully consuming but unproductive member of society. His plan simply gave people more of what helped them and less of what dragged them down.

Similarly, Milton Hershey wasn't interested in offering his chocolatiers a sweet deal at his expense. In his time and place, the only affordable option meant going to the frontier. His plan would work only if he could provide productive workers with a town, or at least a way to get to the factory. Otherwise, who would make the chocolate?

When people are afforded the opportunity to focus freely on their work, and that opportunity is backed by high expectations and appropriate rewards, they'll—guess what?—do their jobs. It's very much in your self interest to create and support a satisfied workforce, because that workforce can build wealth almost as fast as a disgruntled one can destroy it.

Ultimately, the whole thing comes down to the same factors which motivated Fred Smith's pilots at FedEx to gas up company jets with their personal credit cards. Or moved Delta's employees to buy the company an airplane, while Eastern's flight attendants were busily stuffing their faces with food intended for passengers.

*Contented Cows* do give better milk, and better milk translates to better profits. Period. As we continue to make the case with cold, hard facts, and analyze what it takes to create and maintain a capably led, satisfied, highly motivated workforce, expect some holes to be poked in the myths that abound about what employee satisfaction *really* is. We're willing to bet it's probably not what you think.

## CHAPTER SUMMARY

1. Productivity comes from people, not machines.

2. The notion of *Contented Cows* is anything but new—
   we've known for a long time that people can choose to
   contribute if they *want* to.

3. People factors are a source of competitive advantage or
   disadvantage; the choice is yours.

4. Over a 10-year period, the *Contented Cow* companies:

   a. Outgrew the *Common Cows* by a 4:1 margin
      and $111,000 per employee.

   b. Outearned them by nearly $40 billion and
      $384,000 per employee.

   c. Generated a net difference of better than
      800,000 jobs.

5. MVA and EVA evidence is hard to argue with.

6. The argument is for capitalism, not cynicism or
   humanism.

# COWS WITH ATTITUDE

*You can make a happy person into a good worker, but not necessarily the other way around.*

—Gordon Segal – founder, Crate & Barrel

## WHERE DOES CONTENTMENT BEGIN?

We have a healthy suspicion that under your breath right now, you might be muttering things like, "Let's dispense with all this idealistic happy-go-lucky stuff. My employees are what they are. Some of them enjoy working here and give every appearance of being energized by their work, and others don't. They're just not contentable, and I don't see that changing!" You could well be right.

Let's clarify something. The job of "morale maintenance" in your organization does *not* rest entirely on your shoulders, or the shoulders of management in general. But, you'll produce better results if you take reasonable steps that *are* well within your grasp to promote workplace satisfaction.

Managers face at least three challenges with respect to employee motivation and satisfaction (ALL of which involve basic questions about human psychology and its relationship to morale):

1. Hiring people who have the potential to be both productive and satisfied in your specific environment.

2.  Turning the boat around if the majority of the people at work are, shall we say, less than ecstatic already. One way or another, you *do* have to play the hand you were dealt.

3.  Keeping them on track once you get them there.

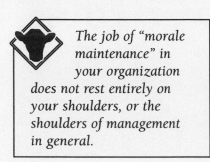

*The job of "morale maintenance" in your organization does not rest entirely on your shoulders, or the shoulders of management in general.*

Do companies see people on the asset or the liability side of the balance sheet? Are employees an opportunity—a source of strategic advantage—or a cost to be reckoned with, and minimized whenever possible? Sadly, most economic and planning models seem to be front-loaded with the assumption that people don't want to work, and won't work without costly stimuli.

## PEACH LIMBS DON'T GROW ON OAKS

A major assumption operating in most businesses is that they exist to make a profit. (At least we know it is in ours.) Hence, almost all of our behavior is in response to that assumption. If we're going to discuss the kinds of practices that will transform your business into a grass-bellied, milk-producing, *Contented Cow*, we first have to deal with the assumptions on which your company operates.

The Coaching Skills training we provide for managers is based in part on the notion that, in order to become more productive, the boss/subordinate relationship needs to be put on more mature footing. Unfortunately, in some organizations, the managerial mindset is still anchored by some deep authoritarian roots; to wit, the change effort is almost certain to fail.

For your practices to be sustainable over time, they must line up with your assumptions. Roosevelt Thomas, founder of

Atlanta's American Institute for Managing Diversity, said it quite succinctly, "Peach limbs don't grow on oaks."[1] He was referring to the fact that a peach limb grafted onto an oak tree will appear to live for a brief time, only to soon die and fall off. You can fake practices you don't believe in for a while, but over the long haul, you won't be able to pull it off.

If you change your employee relations practices without examining the assumptions that drive them, you're certain to be disappointed. In all likelihood, those changes will be arbitrary, weakly executed, short-lived, ineffective, and, worst of all, costly.

> *Fortunately, even when cows are left up to their own devices, they seldom develop poor temperament and vices.*[2]
> —Improving the Welfare of Dairy Cows Through Management

## YOU GET WHAT YOU EXPECT TO GET

So, what do you assume about the people who work in your organization or team? What do you assume about people in general?

If you believe that most people who come to work for you are lazy, stupid, untrustworthy, inept, and just downright contrary, that assumption can't help but show up in the way you run your business. You'll have all kinds of rules and regulations designed for numbskulls who couldn't pour milk out of a boot with the directions printed on the heel. You'll no doubt have a supervisor for every six or seven folks, and will inevitably attract just the kind of people who will live down to your assumptions. Discerning, competent employees won't come anywhere near your place, and your original assumption about people will be reinforced. If you are getting dizzy from the circular nature of all this, let's provide a real, albeit ultra-simple, example.

## A CONSPIRACY AT THE DRY CLEANERS

Prominently displayed on the wall above the phone at my dry cleaners, in full view of everyone, is the following sign:

> **THIS PHONE IS NOT TO BE USED**
> **BY ANYONE FOR ANY REASON**
>
> **THE MANAGEMENT**

One day, being a rather curious sort, I asked one of the employees just what the sign was all about. As has happened on more than one occasion in my adult life, I got that I-can't-believe-you're-asking-such-a-stupid-question look. When pressed for a response, the counter clerk informed me that she had been told in no uncertain terms by the owner, a fellow named Paul, that the sign "meant exactly what it said."

So, I asked another question, "Then why do you have the phone?" Her reply was to the effect that the phone was only to be used for receiving inbound calls from customers. "Do you get many of those calls?" I asked. She indicated that there were only two to three of them per day. And the majority of those calls were from Paul's wife, who, in her words, was "keeping tabs on her husband."

"Then why the rule?" I had to ask.

"I don't know," she said. "I guess Paul doesn't trust us. And I don't know why not."

Which led to my final question. "If I asked to use the phone right now, would you let me?"

"Sure, I don't care. Paul's a jerk, and besides, he's not here now anyhow."

This is a minor example to be sure, but it serves to make a point. You are likely to get just the kind of behavior from employees that you expect. They will either live up or down to your expectations *because* your policies, procedures, and employment practices had at their bedrock those same assumptions.

*I'm not going to have the monkeys running the zoo.*[3]
—Frank Borman, former chairman of Eastern Airlines

## CORE COVENANTS

Organizations operate on a limited number—not a great long list—of core beliefs and assumptions which are burned in to the very fabric of the business. Here are a few you should adopt (seriously) and begin operating on, today.

1. **The Rule of Common Purpose:** The organization must be managed in a way that permits all legitimate stakeholders—managers, employees, owners, and customers to benefit, each in their own way.

2. **The Rule of Selective Membership:** Since the beginning of time, winning organizations the world over have recognized and held dear the notion that membership is a privilege, and not a right. Contrary to popular belief, there really is an ample supply of conscientious, hardworking, capable, honest people. No doubt some of them already work for you. You can (and must) find others like them. You've got to expend a little effort doing it because "eagles don't flock," but they *are* out there. (If you can't accept this notion, sell your business to someone who can, or shut it down now!)

3. **The Rule of Omission:** In the main, your employees, customers, and yes, owners, will be inspired less by what you do *for* them, than by what you *don't* do *to* them. If, for example, you expect them to believe in you and stick with you, never, ever, ever deceive or abuse them! If the company conducts its business in a way that is *sufficiently satisfactory* (you don't have to be Mr. Wonderful) to the people who work there, most of them will perform better, producing more and better stuff.

## BOGUS ASSUMPTIONS

Unfortunately, we have seen too many organizations operating on one or more of the following very erroneous and dangerous assumptions. Watch out!

- That people need paternalistic employers who will take care of them, because they are incapable of taking care of themselves.
- That the more we give people, without expecting anything in return, the happier and better off they'll be.
- That if we run a "kinder, gentler" organization, it will foster love, siblinghood, peace, goodwill, and the world will be a better place to live.

## ASSUMPTIONS ARE A TWO-WAY STREET: THE EMPLOYEES' PERSPECTIVE

The whole subject of assumptions would simplify itself immensely if you only had to mind your own. The problem is everyone else has a set, too. Equally as important as your assumptions about your workforce is the whole question of *their* operative assumptions—about work, the organization, and about you personally.

For example, what are their assumptions about profit? How much is there? Where does it comes from? Where does it go? Given the continuing erosion of the trust factor in the workplace, what are their assumptions when they show up for work in the morning? Are they fully engaged? Or is it more like, "I know they're out to screw me, so I'll get them first?" Do you even know?

What are their assumptions about the organization's priorities right now? Have they had to figure this one out on their own? Or have you told them? Are you sure?

What are their assumptions about you? What's important to you? What do you stand for? Believe in? What will or won't you tolerate? Yes, we know. You probably told everyone this stuff when you hired them, right? But how long ago was that, and have your actions really been consistent with those statements made so long ago?

Unless you and your entire management team have invested considerable personal time and effort communicating honestly and openly—sharing the bad news as well as the good, showing people the numbers, helping them understand them, and making sure that your words are backed up by your actions—you've got people operating with bad data. In other words, your organization very well could be afflicted with a bad case of ignorance, curable, but ignorance nonetheless.

## WHAT EMPLOYEES WANT—THE CONTENTED COWS' VIEW

The view taken by the *Contented Cow* companies seems to be that their employees want (and deserve):

1. **Meaningful Work** – Employees need to feel proud of their work. They want suitable challenges and the freedom to pursue them. They want to be in the game, not on the bench.
2. **High Standards** – They dislike losing organizations and don't want to hang around with losers.
3. **A Clear Sense of Purpose and Direction** – They want to read mysteries, not live them. Timely, relevant, and meaningful (truthful) information is a must.
4. **Balanced "Worth-its"** – A commensurate level of interest and investment in them must be demonstrated. Internal systems which support rather than impede their efforts. Freedom to pursue some things that are important to them.

5. **A Level Playing Field** – Means reciprocal caring, coupled with some sense of justice and an assurance they won't be taken advantage of.
6. **To Be and Feel Competent** – We don't need to explain this one, do we?

## THE "HAPPY CURVE"

Most of this book deals with what happens to people at work, the way they're treated, regarded, related to, and enrolled in the organization's journey. But it's only fair to devote a little attention to a discussion of the importance of "contentability"—the *capacity to be contented*. None of the other ideas and examples we talk about will be of much benefit if you've managed to surround yourself with a herd of irascible beasts.

In an article published in *Business Horizons*, writer Dennis Organ advanced the theory that workplace morale depends not only on the work environment, but to some degree on the internal sense of happiness that employees possess or lack. In other words, hiring inherently happy people can exponentially boost the morale of the organization as a whole.[4]

We think it's a given that to have contented employees, you have to start with "contentable" ones. We've all known people who seem to be happy no matter what, and a few who aren't happy with anything. (For those in the latter category, the organization represents just one more thing to be unhappy about.) So, does job satisfaction depend on what happens to us at work? How we are treated? The so-called working conditions? Or is it an individual's emotional makeup? We think it's both.

Organ's story of Jack Davis makes an interesting case. A former corporate executive, Davis unscientifically formulated the idea of what he called the "Happy Curve," and then came upon some factual basis to back up what he had already figured out intuitively.

First, he noticed that a friend, usually a happy-go-lucky type, seemed to be down in the dumps. One day Davis sat down and talked with him, offering an understanding shoulder and a little encouraging advice. The friend went away refreshed, armed with a few new ideas, and a healthier perspective. It didn't take much to get him back in the saddle. Both knew it would end that way. The friend was just that kind of guy—normally happy, creative, energetic, and lots of fun. He was merely in a slump and needed a boost.[5]

Later, when he took over a company in crisis, Davis found himself with an abundance of opportunities to further test his theory of the "Happy Curve." A nightmare for shareholders, and a really bad place to work, most everyone was miserable, and with good reason. But not everyone. There was a small core of people who were up-beat, supportive, and optimistic, despite the problems around them.

Careful, deliberate observation of these people caused Davis and his staff (none of whom were trained psychologists) to conclude that these folks were just plain, cheerful people, on or off the job. They had stable, fulfilling family lives, interests outside of work, and were confident in their abilities. Ups and downs were a part of their lives too, but on balance, they liked themselves, and they stayed on an even, and relatively elevated, keel.[6]

Now consider the possibility, as Davis did, that each individual has a range of moods. "High" for one person may be "average" for another. Some people would never get as low as others. In fact, each person might have a sort of emotional "setpoint" (like the one that stabilizes our body weight) that their mood tends to gravitate toward, unless something really unusual is going on.[7]

Davis and his crew came to believe that they had somehow ended up with a disproportionately high number of people with relatively low Happy Curves.[8] In other words, the grouches had reached critical mass. Since morale is as much a group dynamic as an individual condition, the large share of low Happy Curves alone was enough to drag down some of the others at least a little.

As time passed, Davis made a conscious effort to hire people who not only were qualified, but seemed in general to have the potential for being happy. While no one was ever fired for being sullen (perhaps they should have been), the organization gradually took on a new, more positive outlook, sales improved, and the spiral turned upward.[9] Of course, higher morale was not the single "silver bullet" that saved this company, but it was an integral factor.

## A STICKY VARIABLE

As it turns out, Davis' experience is corroborated by the results of a number of research studies. What we call "morale" is, according to University of California Berkeley professor Barry Staw, described as a "sticky" variable.[10] That means some of it is accounted for by what is innate about the person, as opposed to environmental factors.

For example, when organizational psychologists measure the job satisfaction of a group of people at two points in time separated by intervals of up to several years, the best and most consistent predictor of job satisfaction at the later time is the earlier assessment of job satisfaction. This finding holds up even when many people in the group have changed jobs or employers. A study of 5,000 adults begun in

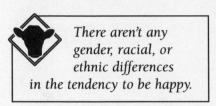

*There aren't any gender, racial, or ethnic differences in the tendency to be happy.*

1973 by the National Institute on Aging found that the happiest of people in that year were still relatively happy 10 years later, regardless of changes in their work or other circumstances.[11]

Perhaps most telling, Staw and his research associates found that a high school counselor's rating of the "cheerfulness" of adolescents predicted their job satisfaction 30 years later as well or better than any single aspect of their jobs![12] Also persuasive are the results of studies of identical twins separated at birth, indicating that 30 percent or more of the variation in adult job satisfaction relates to genetic factors.[13] There might be something to this *sticky* variable business, but of course it's not the whole story. (And if you believe that 30 percent figure, we would guess that's not even half of it.)

We're not saying that work environment doesn't matter. You've had good jobs and bad ones, and you know there's a difference. But we think there's good reason to believe that people do vary in their tendencies to exhibit good morale, within a range, regardless of environmental factors. This in part explains why companies like Southwest Airlines "hire attitudes," preferring to train people in the skills they need. Unfortunately, you can't teach enthusiasm. Any company would do well to adopt a similar philosophy when recruiting.

Despite what you might have heard otherwise, you *can* hire "for fit" and still uphold your organization's commitment to equal employment opportunity. There aren't any gender, racial, or ethnic differences in the tendency to be happy. (The only acceptable discrimination in hiring practices should be directed against grouches!)

## BUT WILL THEY BE CONTENTED HERE?

From the start, we have been making the case that *Contented Cows Give Better Milk*. It's an absolute fact. But it's also a fact that all cows aren't going to be content living on your ranch, so let's be truthful about it. By definition, the *Contented Cow* companies are viewed as exceptional places to work. But that holds true for only certain types of people, and *Contented Cows* unabashedly take steps to ensure that people who won't fit in with their particular environment don't go to work there. (And, if they do

> One measure of a person's capacity to be satisfied and productive at your company is the degree to which they can live with your ground rules.

somehow manage to get on the payroll, that they don't last long!) In effect, what they are recognizing—and it's as true in your company as it is in theirs—is that not everyone would be happy, productive, or successful working there.

As you might guess, they employ a rigorous selection process. Hewlett-Packard candidates have been known to experience eight or more job interviews. Lincoln Electric, the decades-old Cleveland manufacturer of electric motors, reportedly takes it a step further by requiring every new hire to be interviewed and unanimously approved by a board of vice presidents and factory superintendents. Rick and Diane Ernst, who operate one of Alphagraphics' largest and most successful franchises go further still. After conducting an exhaustive recruiting and screening process, they pay potential hires $100 to work with their team

## ALPHAGRAPHICS STORE LOCATIONS

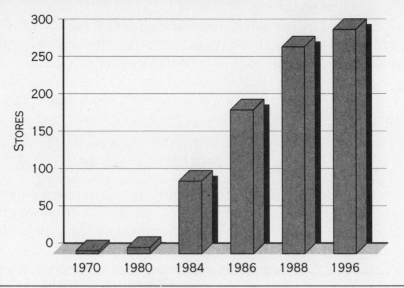

*Source:* Alphagraphics Company Spotlight, 1996

for a day; a measure which gives both parties the opportunity to make an informed decision and opt out, before it's too late. Such measures not only narrow the risk, but also make plain from the very start that the organization is deadly serious about employment matters. It also sends a message to the individual that he or she must be joining an elite organization, thus creating high expectations that in turn breed high performance.

One measure of a person's capacity to be satisfied and productive at your company is the degree to which they can live with your ground rules. Every organization has certain things which are in the realm of the sacrosanct. They are immutable. Changing them is not on the table for discussion. Among other things, *Contented Cow* companies realize the absolute futility of trying to convert someone whose internal compass points 40 degrees to the left of the corporation's. It's not a matter of morality, but makeup. More so than the average company, the *Contented Cow* companies have a crystal clear sense of direction and a keen awareness of their core values. Accordingly, they have little room for those who are unwilling to make the journey with them.

> *Many herds allow their cows to develop their own individual personalities as long as it does not mean special care and treatment. … Individual cows must fit into the system rather than the system conforming to the habits of the cow.*
> —Improving the Welfare of Dairy Cows Through Management

## CHICK-FIL-A: NEVER ON SUNDAY

You can't get a Chick-fil-A chicken sandwich, or anything else on the fast-service chain's menu on a Sunday, because each and every one of their stores is closed that day. If you want to know why, read founder Truett Cathy's book, *It's Easier to Succeed Than to Fail.*

In reality, it doesn't matter why. That's just the way they've chosen to run their business. It stands to reason that they could increase sales by opening their stores on Sunday, but if you want to do it that way, open a McDonald's franchise. Before you assume that they are too old-fashioned for their own good, consider the fact that the majority of Cathy's shopping center-based stores do more business in six days than their food court neighbors do in seven![14]

### CHICK-FIL-A STORE LOCATIONS

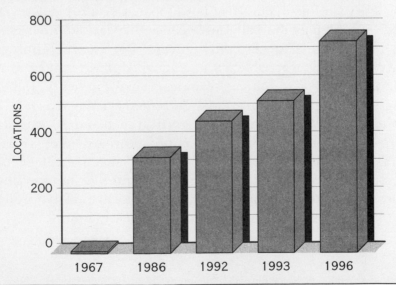

*Source:* Chick-fil-A Annual Message, 1997.

FedEx and Disney, on the other hand, are absolutely fanatical about their corporate appearance. Male applicants who choose to express their individuality by wearing a beard or earring, or women who wear heavy makeup and lots of jewelry shouldn't even slow down as they drive by the gates of either company. As former FedEx Vice President of Personnel Terry Bean used to put it when besieged by the "why can't we wear a beard?" question from the company's 60,000-plus customer contact employees: "You can wear a beard. You just can't do it and work here."

Disney was equally emphatic in 1991 in dealing with a strike by Disneyland employees over the same issue of facial hair. They fired the strike leader. The rest of the "cast" quickly came back to work, and the rule stayed. Any questions? The standards in both cases had been made impeccably clear from the beginning, before anybody was even hired. The company merely lived up to that standard.

For Miami Dolphins' Head Coach Jimmy Johnson, it's an individual's work ethic that counts as much (if not more) than speed or pass catching ability. Johnson has proven it several times over by trading or releasing outright some of the most talented players in the game. Do the names Herschel Walker and Bryan Cox ring a bell? Johnson cut them both loose. Certainly not because they couldn't play football, but because they lacked other essential requirements to play on his team. For Coach Johnson, a player has to be teachable; an unteachable player will be miserable personally and fail the team at crucial moments. Johnson amplifies the point in his book, *Turning the Thing Around*, "We evaluate a helluva lot more than vertical leap and 40-yard dash times. If I'm talking with a group of prospective draftees and one kid's sitting there flipping ice at his teammate, he'll be hard pressed to sit on my list for more than about five more minutes. I have formal training in the psychology of learning, but none of that does any good on an unwilling or uncaring pupil."[15]

*Get good people and expect them to perform. Terminate them quickly and fairly if you make the wrong choice.*[16]

—J. Willard Marriott, Jr.

Time after time, organization after organization, the winners are absolute zealots about who will and won't get to play on their team. At A.G. Edwards, according to CEO Ben Edwards, "We want someone with character who shares our values and who will fit into our culture. We're looking for a long term happy marriage."[17] More often than not, it's the intangible factors rather than raw credentials or ability they most rely on when making that decision. Chick-fil-A has a uniquely positive corporate culture. Operational expertise alone is not enough to cut it there. Truett Cathy says it's as much a person's character as anything else that he looks for when he hires an employee or contracts with an operator for one of his growing number of stores. For him, the fate of the applicant ultimately rests on a single consideration: "Would I like my son or daughter to work for this person?"[18] Their selectivity pays off in more ways than one. Their employee turnover rates, for example, consistently run at less than one-fifth the industry average. From now on, companies will need to reorient their recruitment and selection processes by hiring "for fit" rather than mere credentials or, for that matter, specific job openings.

## CONTENTABILITY AND CORPORATE ASSIMILATION

We know what we've just advocated is that you hire only those people who will be able to *fit in* or assimilate to your culture. And we suspect you may have a problem with organizations that, at least in your eyes, impose "undue" requirements for assimilation. A requirement to assimilate can be a double-edged sword. When organizations require that people fit in around arbitrary or irrelevant considerations, they often filter out potential top performers who don't fit the irrelevant part of their mold. Whenever a company insists that a woman behave like "one of the guys," for example, or that people leave integral aspects of their identity at the door, they're putting the wrong filter on the selection process.

For example, is an inclination or ability to play golf a valid requirement for a job? Well, sure it is for some jobs, like a professional golfer, for instance! Or maybe for a sales position where lots of the company's customers like to do business on the golf course. Then the ability to play golf would be a pretty important job requirement.

I once consulted with a credit card company's vice president of marketing who was trying to pass a guy named Mike off to another department like a hot potato. Mike's "problem" was that he didn't "fit in" to the department. Of course he didn't fit in! Mike was a systems programmer whose job was to design and implement computer software for use by the marketing department. This guy got his kicks writing code in a foreign language and watching it turn into lights on a screen. He was a genius! He had developed some of the slickest stuff any of us had ever seen. Unmarried, he spent more than 60 hours at his terminal every week, both at the office and at home. I learned that the reason he didn't fit in was that he didn't drink and he didn't play golf. (*It's amazing how those two activities go hand-in-hand.*) Incredulous, I asked sarcastically, "What do you need, a wine-taster, or a computer guy!??" The veep was about to cast off one of his greatest assets, for a reason that amounted, in real terms, to nothing.

The other edge of this sword is that strong leaders of outstanding organizations realize that many people, regardless of talent, will not be able to meet the requirements necessary to succeed in their *Contented Cow* companies. It's not that they can't do the work, but that they won't be happy, productive, or successful working there. What sets these companies apart, though, is that they are actually doing something about the realization. Their assimilation criteria are strictly business-oriented, deliberate, and rational, and do not consist of conveniences, preferences, or unquestioned traditions.

To be sure, every organization requires some degree of assimilation. You must be completely in touch with the real requirements for success in your business, and highly disciplined in proclaiming those things loudly, clearly, and unashamedly to all who would invest their time and hopes in working there. Ultimately, as Roosevelt Thomas puts it, "There will always be a need for some assimilation. People will always have to salute certain organizational flags. The job of the leader is to be very clear about which flags need to be saluted."[19]

Company standards and assimilation criteria exist for a reason, and frequently, it begins with the letter "C," for Customer. Concerning the beard issue at FedEx, for example, the message they've gotten loud and clear from literally hundreds of focus group sessions with their customers is that they prefer a neatly attired, clean-cut look. The way the company sees it, as much money as you're paying to do business with them, they're only too happy to oblige.

Disney is every bit as emphatic about the use of coarse language. But if you fathom the simple logic behind Disney's requirement, it has a lot to do with the fact that the majority of what they sell is based on an image of clean, wholesome entertainment for some very impressionable kids.

It's no less the case at Marriott, where only about 10 percent of job applicants meet the company's requirements. If an applicant is at all uncomfortable with their clean-living, extremely service-conscious environment, he/she will not make it there. Some would say that the Marriott Way has its roots in the company's Mormon-influenced origins. Maybe so. But as frequent Marriott guests, we can tell you that wherever it comes from, it most assuredly makes a difference. Ditto for others like J&J, HP, Nordstrom, and Procter & Gamble.

## THE PROOF IS IN THE PEOPLE

Having put forth some of the behavioral drivers behind the best stool-and-bucket *Contented Cow* companies, let's describe three very fundamental characteristics they share regarding their employment practices. Are you ready? The rest of this book is going to hang on these three branches (no speed-reading).

While the *Contented Cow* companies are unique in many ways, they share remarkable commonality in three important respects. Day in and day out, *each* of them does a remarkable job of:

1. Getting (and keeping) their people solidly lined up behind the organization's core purpose and objectives. In short, they're **Committed**.
2. Letting people know through a myriad of ways, some large (but mostly small), that they're important. They're more than just a number or body. They are **Cared About**: first as people, then as professionals.
3. Through personal as well as systemic means, removing the obstacles from the path of their workforce. In short, they have **Enabled** their people to perform.

Analyzing each of these areas in the chapters to come, we'll address the following questions:

1. What exactly are the components of these characteristics? How will you recognize it when you see them?
2. How can you replicate it? Here, we'll look at two aspects of the equation:
   a. Employee relations practices – These are obviously (we think they're obvious) those things you actually do to promote contentment and productivity. You know—pay, benefits, employee involvement, team-

work, the hiring and decision-making processes—all of them—and more.

b.  Operational practices – All the decisions you make about running the business which aren't directed at employee relations—but that employees nonetheless must depend on or contend with. These are less obvious, because they won't come up in a discussion of employee relations, but they have a tremendous effect on contentedness, and on frustration levels. Things like customer service policies, safety, equipment maintenance, etc.

3.  What are the employees' responsibilities? What must people do to ensure their own contentment? This is anything but a one-way street.

4.  Finally, to help you three-dimensionalize the ideas governing each chapter, we'll identify some of the people and organizations that are doing an especially good job in these areas. From time to time, we'll also take a look at those which have "climbed the mountain" but, due to a failed strategy in other respects, have lost ground, money, or ceased to exist altogether.

Our job, then, will be to pick through the situations and examples, bringing to light those which define each characteristic in the simplest, clearest, and most replicable manner.

## CHAPTER SUMMARY

1. Just as they affect virtually every other outcome in our lives, our assumptions about people (their relative good or bad qualities, and their propensity to work without first being threatened) drive our employee relations practices, and in turn, the outcome of the relationship. You get what you expect. Practices that are inconsistent with your organization's operating assumptions are doomed to fail.

2. Never lose sight, even for a moment, of the expectations of employees in a *Contented Cow* company, most notably their requirements for:
   - meaningful work
   - high standards
   - clear purpose and direction
   - balanced "worth-its"
   - a level playing field
   - being and feeling competent

3. Similarly, don't allow yourself to become distracted by the bogus assumptions that are often put before us, particularly those advocating "kinder and gentler" standards (or no standards at all); blatant paternalism; or the need to give or pay more without good and compelling reasons.

4. Hire "for fit," and not just talent. Make sure the *fit* requirements are relevant to business success.

5. Face it, not everyone's going to be content "living on your ranch."

6. Contented Cows are:
   - **Committed**
   - **Cared About**
   - **Enabled**

# SECTION TWO

## CONTENTED COWS ARE COMMITTED

# THE "VISION THING" ... PASSENGERS OR CREW

*It doesn't take a genius to figure out that in an environment where there is a shared vision of excellence ... where people can be the best they can be on a daily basis ... where, when they know what is expected of them ... understand that reward is linked to performance ... and BELIEVE they can make a difference because they will be heard ... they WILL make a difference. They will go BEYOND our expectations and great things will start to happen.*[1]

—FedEx founder and CEO Frederick W. Smith

## JUST ALONG FOR THE RIDE

Not long ago, we met with a business unit training manager for one of the world's largest telecommunications companies. This individual, who had expressed an interest in some of the training we do, had been with the company in the same location for 19 years and had worked in almost every staff department under the roof. Following our customary routine, we asked her, "What kind of training do you currently provide for the employees here?" Her answer, sounding like something straight out of a departmental policy manual was, "Oh, whatever kind of training they need to make and deliver our products." Because of the breadth and complexity of her company's operations (and the fact that this was our first meeting with her), it seemed reasonable to ask, "And what products do you make and deliver here?"

"I knew you were going to ask me that," she said. "To be honest with you, I couldn't tell you. I don't have any idea." Needless to say, we were more than a little dumbfounded to hear a 19-year veteran whose whole professional life had been with the same employer—which was not the CIA—admit to being totally ignorant about where her paycheck came from. How in the world can she possibly be contributing, let alone doing a good job? How can her daily actions result in anything other than an impediment to the organization's success? Some might suggest that this is such an extreme example as to border on the ridiculous. We'd like to believe that, but we're not so sure.

## DESTINATION UNKNOWN?

Billions are spent every year on internal corporate communications, including $50 million-plus by the above-referenced company. Even so, most organizations still do a miserable job of helping their folks understand the direction, goals, and priorities of the business (let alone securing their Commitment to them). If you doubt the magnitude of this "failure to communicate" claim, take five minutes and go do some field research of your own. Ask a sample of your people to jot down what *they* believe to be the organization's three highest priorities and where they think it is headed. When the answers come back without any degree of consistency, the question is obvious: *If they don't know where you're going, how can they possibly help you get there?*

## BURNING OFF THE FOG

Clearly, in some companies people seem to "get it," and in others they don't. We wanted to know what makes the difference. If your people know (*really* know) what the organization is all about, how did they find out? What did you have to do?

We asked these questions of almost everyone we came in contact with while writing this book. Aside from the fact that most leaders simply didn't have an answer, the few who did offered nothing terribly new or complicated. We had hoped to hear of some ingenious, idiot-proof techniques guaranteed to inject the milk of human understanding into every living thing under the corporate roof. We didn't find any. But what we *did* hear over and over from organizations whose people do seem to "get it" and "get it good" is that you simply tell them, and show them by practically "carpet bombing" people from day one with the same simple, clear-cut, credible message.

In a survey of senior executives at 86 major firms, respondents told Mercer Management Consulting, Inc. that half their employees couldn't even articulate the corporate strategy. (*We'd like to meet the half who could.*) Mercer's study found one reason for this shortcoming was that the business strategy and direction had been set at a level too far over the heads of people at the operating level. Any sense of ownership or degree of understanding on their part was virtually precluded.[2] We submit there are at least four more reasons which explain this phenomenon:

**1. The Event Syndrome.** In all too many cases, the attempt to communicate these priorities, goals, etc., takes place only once a year, or maybe every three or four years, usually after some mountain-top retreat or strategic planning session. A wonderfully crafted letter, speech, pamphlet, or video is produced. Everyone endures the obligatory viewing, and then promptly goes back to what they were doing, safely assured that the topic won't come up again for at least another year.

In one organization familiar to us, the senior management group returned from its three-day, mountain-top experience in "Moses-like" fashion, bearing (*get this*) stone tablets with the newly minted corporate goals inscribed on them. With phrases like "competitively superior, highly integrated, broad-based networks" inscribed on the tablets, we're fairly certain that more than a few of their people couldn't even pronounce some of this stuff, let alone understand or remember it. Fortunately, those rocks made pretty good paperweights.

**2. Message of the Week.** In other cases, companies somehow expect all those thoughtful, intelligent people they call employees to buy the notion that this week they're a "Market Leader," knowing all the while that next week they'll be the "Most Operationally Efficient," "Lowest Cost Producer," or something else. Come on, get real! It's almost as if many executives are suffering from the very same Attention Deficit Disorder that grips a lot of of our school-age children. (Maybe there should be a Ritalin Rx for the boardroom.)

3. **"Watch Their Bellybutton" or "Talk is Cheap."** Early in their careers, basketball players are taught that one of the best ways to anticipate movement when guarding an opponent is to watch their midsection, as it reliably predicts where the rest of the person is going. The same thing is true off the court, as well. Too often, what our people see is our bellybutton going one way and our mouth another.

4. **Mission Statement vs. Sense of Mission.** Comparatively speaking, executives spend entirely too much time and precious energy crafting precisely worded mission, vision, and value statements relative to the effort they invest in making darned sure every human being on their payroll truly understands and appreciates what all that stuff means.

*Executives spend entirely too much time and precious energy crafting precisely worded mission, vision, and value statements relative to the effort they invest in making darned sure every human being on their payroll truly understands and appreciates what all that stuff means.*

In case after case, the *Contented Cow* companies are the ones doing the best job of helping their people see, feel, and appreciate where the business is headed, why it is going there, and what role they are expected to play. While their efforts aren't usually the slickest or fanciest (no stone tablets to be sure), they are clear, consistent, and "udderly" compelling.

*A leader has got to show his troops the route of the march and the destination.*[3]

—Frank Pacetta, Xerox Sales Manager

## EYE ON RETAIL: WHAT HAPPENED?

It's impossible to talk about the retail sector without examples from companies like Wal-Mart and Sears—the really big merchandisers—dominating the discussion. While each operates in this brutally competitive arena, there are some distinct differences, both on and off the income statement. Together they accounted for $117 billion in combined annual revenues in 1995. However, as Figures 3.1 and 3.2 indicate, the commonality between them may end with the T-shirts, car batteries, and housewares which each of them sells.

While our intent is not to malign Sears (or any other company), the fact remains that they have had their problems, both in the boardroom and in their stores. Largely, these problems stemmed from an arrogance displayed toward both customers and employees, but not necessarily in that order. In 1989, Sears' Allstate Insurance unit (the "Good Hands People") effectively cratered relations with its sales force by unilaterally imposing de facto sales quotas—a move that spawned widespread defections, and, according to some, questionable underwriting practices. Ditto for its auto repair unit, where in the early '90s, a new compensation scheme sparked complaints of unnecessary repairs and

---

**FIGURE 3.1**

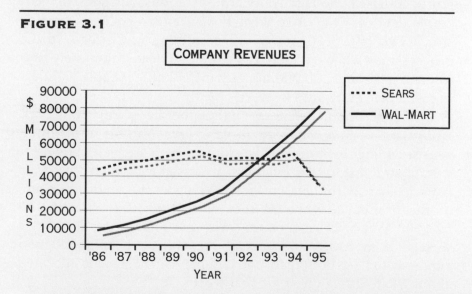

**FIGURE 3.2**

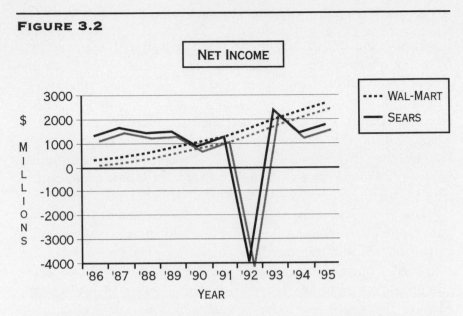

NET INCOME

overcharges, causing the company to pay out millions to settle claims in California and New Jersey.[4]

Sears' inability to effectively decide, let alone communicate, what business it was in resulted in the closure or sale of its Cold-well Banker Real Estate operations, Dean Witter, Eye Care Centers of America, the Discover Card operations, Allstate, the venerable catalog (*America's Wish Book*), and associated catalog stores. Even the Sears Tower office building in Chicago. In the process, they whacked more than 100,000 heads from their payroll and left some 360,000 not especially happy people wondering who or what would be next.

Wal-Mart and J.C. Penney, on the other hand, have long been recognized as companies which go to great lengths to maintain a satisfied, highly motivated workforce. Both are well known for having straightforward business philosophies which they take pains to share with their workforce, along with a handsome share of the profits. Nowhere is this more evident than with the 622,000 Wal-Mart "associates" who participate regularly in a variety of meetings and special recognition events designed expressly to keep both them and company management informed about what's going on in the real world.

Keep in mind that communicating with the Wal-Mart workforce is no mean feat. First, as we have already mentioned, there are more than a half million people to communicate with. Second, consider the fact that their workforce is comprised largely of second career mothers, senior citizens, and teenagers. (Imagine trying to have a business-related conversation with *your* adolescent son or daughter.)

But communicate they do. According to the late Sam Walton, founder of Wal-Mart, "It all comes down to how well [we] can communicate and truly be sincere in helping [our] associates understand what our basic philosophy is, and what our

> *You have got to work in their best interest ... you have got to put their interest first, and eventually it will come back to the company.*

basic goals are, and involving them in our business. ... I guess our greatest technique and our greatest accomplishment is this commitment to communicating with them in every way that we possibly can, and listening to them constantly. I think every good company has got to have that kind of aura, have a partnership relationship, really, with their employees. You have got to work in their best interest. ... You have got to put their interest first, and eventually it will come back to the company."[5]

## GETTING THE CUSTOMER-FOR-LIFE TREATMENT

Walton is absolutely right. The demonstrated commitment does "come back to the company" through Wal-Mart employees like Lisa (not her real name), who works in the jewelry department of a store near my home. In search of a battery for my wife's watch, I stopped at Lisa's store after visiting Sears, where I had been shrugged off with a curt, "Nope, we don't have it. Nope, we don't carry the watch. Nope, we don't know where you can get one." (Sears originally started out as the R.W. Sears Watch company. Ironic, huh?)

Although Wal-Mart didn't have a new battery either, Lisa managed to find a used one with some charge left in a box of spare watch parts. Because the timepiece had been purchased elsewhere (Wal-Mart did not even carry the brand), Lisa informed me she'd be happy to give me the battery, but that I would have to install it myself. She was prohibited from working on watches the store didn't carry, just in case a repair went wrong and a replacement could not be offered. After watching all 10 of my thumbs struggling to crack open the back of this tiny ladies' dress watch and install a battery the size of a BB, Lisa cautiously but confidently intervened. She did what you should want your employees to do, even in the face of a policy to the contrary.

So, what was the net of this transaction? First, it would have been far easier and safer for Lisa to do nothing, like her Sears counterpart, rather than spend half an hour with someone not even making a purchase and defy a store policy in the process. Wal-Mart didn't recognize one dime in revenue from the deal *on that particular day*, but they did get what Texas car dealer Carl Sewell has termed a Customer for Life—a customer they will make plenty of money from over the years.

Perhaps the better question is *why* did this happen? What is it that Wal-Mart knows that Sears managed to forget in its storied 110-year past? Somehow, somewhere along the way, in a Wal-Mart store meeting, or one of those goofy pep rallies we've all heard about, or in the course of a conversation with her manager, or more probably *all* of the above, Lisa got the message that even at the ripe old age of 20, her opinion mattered. She was secure in the knowledge that as long as she was looking out for a customer and doing what she felt to be right, she was not only permitted but expected to use her own best judgment, *even if it meant contradicting a policy decree from some vice-president in Bentonville, Arkansas*. Her counterparts at Sears, on the other hand, had fallen victim to a culture so authoritarian that someone in Sears management actually felt they needed three pages of policy guidelines to clarify how and when people were to take coffee breaks![6]

## MOMENTS OF TRUTH

In his 1987 book *Moments of Truth*, SAS Airline President Jan Carlzon suggested that it is in these fleeting moments of interaction between customers and front-line employees that the fate of any customer-driven organization is determined. Speaking of SAS, he said, "If we are truly dedicated to orienting our company toward each customer's individual needs, then we cannot rely on rule books and instructions from distant corporate offices. We have to place responsibility for ideas, decisions, and actions with the people who are SAS during those brief seconds."[7]

To be sure, Carlzon was not advocating that businesses be run simply on the whims of whatever each individual employee happens to feel like doing at the moment. There needs to be some form of structure and decision-making process. But, like Sam Walton, he is suggesting that in many organizations the gulf that exists between a truly involved workforce hitting on all cylinders, and one that gives every appearance of being brain dead can be best bridged with credible information—artfully presented and continually reinforced—about **where** the organization is going, **why** it's going there, what it stands for, and **what** it needs and expects from all hands on deck. Good, timely information enables people to perform at a higher rate of speed and with fewer errors. Without that information, they must inevitably slow down to sort things out.

Walk into *The Sandwich Store*, a nondescript little deli in Jacksonville, Florida, and within nanoseconds you'll realize that you are in the presence of four people who are absolutely on a mission. That mission, which each of them has so clearly embraced, is to "serve lunch fast!" The food is good, very good, in fact, but what's really impressive is the speed with which Renee Curry, the thirtysomething owner of the shop, and her three co-workers can make a sandwich, fill a soft drink cup, ring up an order, get it all correct, and get people on their way somewhere between 300–400 times per day!

These folks are focused like a laser on that objective, and execute so well that we would highly recommend the place to the industrial engineers at McDonald's and Burger King who could no doubt learn a thing or two. Sometimes getting the message of "what we're all about" across to the troops is a simple matter of telling them clearly and showing them *consistently*. As Carlzon puts it, "Setting a good example is truly the most effective means of communication—and setting a poor one is disastrous!"[8] This is clearly a lesson not lost on Renee.

## THERE IS NO SUCH THING AS OVER COMMUNICATION

In 1995, the Families and Work Institute conducted a survey in which they asked people, "Besides compensation, what else is important in your job?" The number one answer, besting such predictable responses as job security, nature of the work, and "my supervisor," was open communication.[9] People want you to tell them what they need to know to do their jobs.

We talked with David Graham, CEO of InTuition, Inc., a privately-held, 500-employee company that provides data and other services to the student loan industry. We wanted to find out how InTuition took a four million dollar loss in 1991—the year Graham and his partners took over the management of the company (which they later bought)—and turned the red ink into four million in profits five years later. Not surprisingly, his answer was "our people." But when we probed a little further, we found that this relatively small *Contented Cow* company really *had* been able to rebuild largely on the back of an inspired workforce.

From whence came the inspiration? Information. "Because we think it [communication] is so important," says Graham, "we've made it company policy to create as many opportunities and mechanisms for communication as possible. There's no such thing as over communication."[10]

At InTuition, communication starts with a three-day orientation. Normally, we are not big fans of orientations, at least in the traditional sense, because most of them have been reduced to mindless drivel and filling out forms. But we like what happens at InTuition's orientations and afterward. Together with COO Claude Collier, Graham talks with new hires about InTuition's relatively short but checkered history, its culture, and everyone's mutual expectations. Then, a few months later, they reassemble the orientation group for an "Orientation Reunion." Graham and Collier then sit down with the reunited group and ask, "Okay, here's what we promised you on the day you started. Where have we hit the mark, and where have we missed it?" They listen and then get to work addressing any deficiencies or inconsistencies.[11]

And that's only the beginning. Once a week, Graham and Collier each try to take an employee to lunch, just to hear what's going on. Once every month, people are chosen randomly to meet for lunch with the CEO. One of the topics up for discussion is "What do you like (not like) about the way things work around here?" Each of the company's three divisions also meets independently every month to discuss what's happening internally in their division. David and Claude join these meetings to fill them in about what's going on in the other two divisions.

> *A company cannot possibly hire enough managers and issue enough policy manuals to get all its employees to do what it wants them to do!*

At SAS Institute, the software developer outside of Raleigh, North Carolina (no relation to SAS Airlines of Sweden), Public Affairs Manager Les Hamashima apparently knows that in order for employees to understand and truly accept the mission of the company, the inculcation process will take time and lots of it. They don't try to imprint the mission of SAS onto the minds of new employees and expect them to be able to appreciate it right away. It is a process that takes much more than one day of orientation and the memorization of the mission statement. It is something that can only be built through day-to-day interaction with fellow SAS employees who are already living the mission. The values of the company—that the company exists because of the customer—become apparent by the examples other employees set.

## SAS INSTITUTE REVENUE

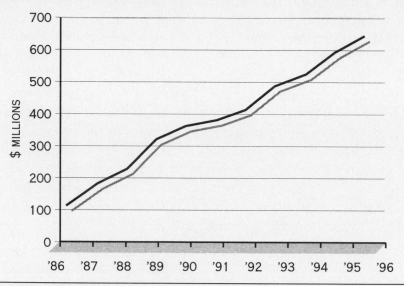

*Source:* SAS Institute Corporation and Financial Results, 1997.

Regardless of where people get the "word," without it a company cannot *possibly* hire enough managers and issue enough policy manuals to get all its employees to do what it wants them to do! Just ask someone like U.S. Postmaster General Marvin Runyon, who has the unenviable task of righting an organization that has tried it the other way around. Yet no matter what size the company, if the words on the mission statement do not match the reality of the work environment, employees will turn cynical and regard management's efforts as only so much corporate propaganda. Most importantly, their Commitment will not be forthcoming. Good information will determine whether the people in your organization, or any organization, are going to be truly Committed to a common purpose, or merely compliant with orders from above and just along for the ride.

## HIGH EXPECTATIONS BEGET
## HIGH PERFORMANCE

When it comes to Commitment, there is no middle ground. People are either passengers or they're crew. They are either Committed (yes, that's with a capital "C") or they are not. If they fall into the latter category, as much as you might want to believe otherwise, it's probably not because *they're* stupid, lazy, or mean-spirited. Certainly, a few are, but in the main, people perform the way they do because we haven't done *our* part as leaders to get them enrolled for the journey. (Remember, you get what you expect.)

To do that, we have to show them the *big picture*. According to Jack Stack, who brought Springfield Remanufacturing back from the brink, "The big picture is all about motivation. It's giving people the reason for doing the job, the purpose of working. If you're going to play a game, you have to understand what it means to win. When you show people the big picture, you define winning."[12]

In a 1994 employee opinion survey involving nearly 80,000 people from a multitude of companies, employees were asked whether or not upper management provided them ample information about the company's goals. Fairly straightforward question, right? Well, in the minds of more than 40 percent of the respondents, the answer was "no." Now, if you put any credence at all in Jack Stack's experience, that suggests that in at least 40 percent of those cases, people had no hope whatsoever of winning. Face it, if we cannot or will not give our folks straightforward information about where the ship is headed, how can we *possibly* ask them to sign on?

High expectations create an environment where both individual and company growth can occur. Each and every one of us wants desperately to be a winner. No one gets up in the morning and says to themselves, "I want to go LOSE today." However, people often don't know *how* to win in their jobs. Therefore, they either have to be shown, or else everyone loses while managers stand idly by. Too often, "winning" is defined in terms that are overly dry (does the name Bob Dole mean anything to you?);

sterile (take a look at your own company's strategic plan or "vision statements"); or completely irrelevant to the intended audience (Company X wants to achieve ROCE of 16.2 percent). **Come on, get real!!!** Dr. Martin Luther King Jr. didn't launch an entire movement with the words, "I have a strategic plan!"

## CHAPTER SUMMARY

1. *Contented Cows* are *Committed Cows*.

2. Employees won't part with their "discretionary effort" for just any old reason. They must have what they consider to be good and compelling reasons. The "cause" must be impeccably clear, incredibly compelling, and it's got to square with their sensibilities.

3. Far too few employees know what the company does, where it's going, what it stands for, believes in, and where they fit in.

4. When it comes to Commitment, there's no middle ground—you either are or you aren't.

5. Committed employees are the only ones capable of delivering the kind of quality and service needed to compete.

6. Managers in the *Contented Cow* companies communicate, through word and deed, in every way imaginable, what the company is all about. The word "overcommunication" isn't even in their lexicon.

7. High expectations beget high performance.

# THE PATH TO COMMITMENT

*When the organization has a clear sense of its purpose, direction, and desired future state, and when this image is widely shared, individuals are able to find their own roles both in the organization and the larger society of which they are a part. They gain a sense of importance as they are transformed from robots blindly following instructions to human beings engaged in a creative and purposeful venture.*
—Bennis, Warren & Nanus, Burt - *Leaders*

## SO WHAT SHOULD YOU DO TO GET PEOPLE COMMITTED?

We believe there are four specific information needs to be met to achieve high levels of employee Commitment. In short, these are things your employees need, want, and have a right to know:

## 1. WHAT IS THIS COMPANY ALL ABOUT?

Your people need to know what the organization stands for and what it believes in. What is *really* important? What kinds of things, if they do them, will get them promoted? What'll get them fired? No, they do not want a long list of rules and regulations, or the type of pablum put out by your PR or HR department, just the plain, unadulterated facts.

## No IDENTITY CRISIS AT J&J

One organization which has demonstrated clear and consistent superiority communicating its identity is Johnson & Johnson. In a short, 308-word document known simply as "The Credo,"* they have effectively articulated just about everything anyone needs to know about what the company stands for and deems important. The Credo isn't something they cooked up just last week. It has been around about as long as their Band-Aids (since 1943 to be exact). Although it is subjected to regular internal review, scarcely a word of it has ever been changed. While many companies may have such hallowed documents stashed away in their vaults, it is doubtful that any could demonstrate as convincingly as J&J has that they actually mean it and believe what's printed on the paper.

J&J openly discusses their Credo with prospective employees, makes sure new hires get a copy of it, publishes it on the cover of their annual reports, and most importantly, they *live* it. Like in 1982, when the company successfully dealt with one of the greatest corporate crises in modern times: the Tylenol scare.

## *JOHNSON & JOHNSON'S CREDO

> *We believe our first responsibility is to the doctors, nurses and patients, to mothers and fathers and all others who use our products and services. In meeting their needs everything we do must be of high quality. We must constantly strive to reduce our costs in order to maintain reasonable prices. Customers' orders must be serviced promptly and accurately. Our suppliers and distributors must have an opportunity to make a fair profit.*

> *We are responsible to our employees, the men and women who work with us throughout the world. Everyone must be considered as an individual. We must respect their dignity and recognize their merit. They must have a sense of security in their jobs. Compensation must be fair and adequate, and working conditions clean, orderly and safe. We must be mindful of ways to help our employees fulfill their family responsibilities. Employees must feel free to make suggestions and complaints. There must be equal opportunity for employment, development and advancement for those qualified. We must provide competent management, and their actions must be just and ethical.*

*We are responsible to the communities in which we live and work and to the world community as well. We must be good citizens - support good works and charities and bear our fair share of taxes. We must encourage civic improvements and better health and education. We must maintain in good order the property we are privileged to use, protecting the environment and natural resources.*

*Our final responsibility is to our stockholders. Business must make a sound profit. We must experiment with new ideas. Research must be carried on, innovative programs developed and mistakes paid for. New equipment must be purchased, new facilities provided and new products launched. Reserves must be created to provide for adverse times. When we operate according to these principles, the stockholders should realize a fair return.*

*Source:* 1996 Johnson & Johnson Annual Report

By his own admission, former J&J CEO Jim Burke spent upwards of 40 percent of his time communicating the Credo— not developing it, explaining it! While some might find it excessive for a CEO to spend that much of his or her time engaged in communicating what the organization stands for and where it's going, we would argue that it's the single most important job they've got!

According to Burke, "All of our management is geared to profit on a day-to-day basis. That's part of the business of being in business. But too often, in this and other businesses, people are inclined to think, 'We'd better do this because if we don't, it's going to show up on the figures over the short-term.' This document allows them to say, 'Wait a minute. I don't have to do that.' The management has told me that they're interested in operating under this set of principles, so I won't."[1]

Some might think it a little odd that only in the fourth (and final) paragraph does J&J's Credo refer to the company's obligations to its stockholders. The first three paragraphs deal with topics like customers, employees, and the communities of which they are a part. But before you start feeling too sorry for their stockholders, take a look at *Fortune's* 1996 "Most Admired List" (J&J ranks fourth); *Business Week's* 1996 list of "Most Valuable

Companies" (J&J ranks eighth); and the fact that between 1985 and 1995, J&J earned an eye-popping average annual return to investors of 23.1 percent.

## IN THE HAY AT KINGSTON

While communicating the what-we're-all-about message can be as simple as telling employees clearly and showing them *consistently*, remember, they'll be watching your bellybutton. The corporate bellybutton is precisely what the 527 employees of Kingston Technologies in Fountain Valley, California—the world's largest manufacturer of computer memory and enhancement products—were watching when Kingston founders David Sun and John Tu sold the company in August, 1996 to Softbank Corp. of Japan. The employees were not relegated to the status of observers for long, however, as Sun and Tu forked over $40 million in bonuses to them. The bonuses resulted in an average distribution of more than $75,000 per employee, with some people earning as much as $300,000![2]

Upon hearing Kingston's story, everyone's first reaction is, "I'd be committed too, for those bucks!" But the point, argue the founders, is that the bonuses were the *effect* of the high commitment, not its cause, which is perfectly consistent with the company's espoused beliefs: "Kingston's culture is 'employees are number one,'" says Sun. "If we can bring the employees together, then you win the customer everywhere."[3]

To be sure, Sun and Tu had no more obligation to share the wealth than their employees did to part with copious amounts of their own discretionary effort in the first place. Yet part with it they did, like the Kingston technician who flew from sunny California to snowy New York for the weekend to repair a system problem. Okay, that much was his job. But when the problem turned out to be a minor, 15-minute fix, rather than taking off for the rest of the weekend, the technician decided to stay and help the customer with some other computer glitches he was experiencing. "My return ticket wasn't 'til Sunday night anyway," he reasoned, knowing his conscientious actions "above and beyond" duty's call had made the company a Kingston customer for life.

Conscientious employees at Kingston seem to be the rule rather than the exception. Take the service call which came into Kingston's Fountain Valley office from a Southern California hotel customer one evening about 6:30. The caller explained that the hotel was in a real pickle, but they couldn't afford to bring the whole system down until after two the next morning. They had to keep the reservations system available, or lose tons of money. The Kingston employee, a fairly new recruit, took it upon himself to go home for a few hours and get some sleep. Then he got up at 1:00 A.M. and drove to the hotel, where he stayed up all night and fixed the problem at a time when it was convenient for the customer. To top it off, he showed up on time for work the next morning and worked his full schedule. Did he have to do that? Of course not, no more than Sun and Tu had to pay out the big bonuses. See? What goes around really does come around.

## "SELLIN' CHICKEN"

The mission at Chick-fil-A is about as clear and uncomplicated as it gets. While I was conducting a Coaching Skills workshop at the company's headquarters near the Atlanta airport, one class-member volunteered that "[Founder and CEO] Truett Cathy has always been very clear about what we do here at Chick-fil-A: *We sell chicken.* It's as simple as that. And no matter what you're doing, if it pertains to *sellin' chicken*, then you're probably doing the right thing. If whatever you're doing gets in the way of *sellin' chicken*, or if it doesn't have anything to do with *sellin' chicken*, you better not let Truett find out about it. And he finds out about everything."

Truett Cathy never saw any reason to micro-manage. For nearly 50 years he had been very clear. In simple, easy-to-understand terms, he told people that as long as their activities promoted *sellin' chicken*—within the parameters of the company's unusually high standard of ethics—it was sanctioned, condoned, and encouraged. That answered a lot of questions, and eliminated the need for a lot of hefty "Sears-like" policy manuals.

At one point in the workshop, I accompanied a small group from the class to a breakout room on another floor. As the elevator door opened, there stood Truett, on his way up to his office from the basement. After warm greetings to each of the seminar participants by name and an introduction to me, whom he didn't know from Adam's house cat, he asked interestedly, "Whatchall doin'?" They all chimed in chorus, *"Sellin' chicken!"* Truett beamed, and he probed no further.

## 2. WHERE ARE WE GOING AND WHY?

People want to know what journey you are asking them to sign up for. Do you plan to go to the moon by the end of the decade? The White House in 2001? Ten billion dollars in revenue by the year 2000? The Super Bowl in five years? Or what? Sadly, most organizations fail and fail miserably on this one. They either have no credible sense of mission, or they can't articulate it. Either way, it spells disaster.

If people don't know full well where your ship is headed, they can't possibly help you get there. Talking about this very task at GE, Jack Welch said that the company must "define its destiny in broad but clear terms. You need an overarching message, something big, but simple and understandable."[4] Howard Putnam (former Southwest Airlines president and CEO) explained the very practical implications of the problem: "Most companies fail in their growth because they don't have a vision. They don't know where to go. When you have a vision and someone comes to you with some convoluted idea, you can hold it up to the vision and ask "Does it fit? Does it fly? If not, don't bother me." A vision must be so strong that it can outweigh the egos of managers that might want to take off in a different direction."[5]

*Where there is no vision, the people perish.*
—Franklin D. Roosevelt

## LOST IN SPACE

Over its course in history of being both a winning and later a losing organization, NASA has exemplified the importance of the sense of mission perhaps better than anyone. Following President Kennedy's declaration that the nation would put a man on the moon and return him safely to Earth by the end of the decade, the thousands of men and women who make up NASA proceeded to do the very best work of their professional lives in order to make that dream a reality.

Once the "moonshot" had been accomplished, however, no goal as compelling was put in its place, and the agency lost sight of where it was going. Tragically, as evidenced by the space shuttle *Challenger* disaster, we all know where it went.

## GUARANTEEING A WIN

One of the hands-down winners in the world of sports has got to be Jimmy Johnson, the former head coach of the Dallas Cowboys who currently holds the same position with the Miami Dolphins. When he took over an ailing Cowboys team in 1989, Johnson proclaimed that in five years the team would be going to the Superbowl. How's that for mission clarity? Johnson didn't say they would be going to the playoffs, win the division, or settle for a winning record. Nothing less than the Superbowl would do. Although Johnson misspoke (it only took four years), the lesson for us is that because the mission was Bold, Clear, and Meaningful, it was also compelling. It captured the hearts and minds not just of a football franchise, but an entire city.

Speaking about his bold public statements prior to the 1990, 1991, and 1992 seasons, Johnson said, "All three times the media looked at me like 'this guy's nuts.' But all three times, our players got a message that was strong and positive about high expectations, and all three times they lived up to the expectations."[6] The importance of the part about high expectations cannot be overstated. People who show up for work at your place or ours have a need for some very basic— and affordable—things, and one of them is the opportunity to do meaningful and significant work. Modest expectations inspire modest work!

## THE CRAYON TEST

In his book, *Beating the Street*, former Fidelity Magellan Fund manager Peter Lynch makes the case that investors ought not put their money into anything which "cannot be explained with a crayon."[7] Given the complexity of today's financial markets, that's probably good advice. It is every bit as useful, however, for those of us who are entrusted with explaining to others where our organization is headed. If you can't convey that message, graphically and credibly, with the very same crayon (literally), then you can't explain it, and your people ought not (and probably won't) invest in it!

Once the journey and its purpose have been made impeccably clear, however, it's time for everyone (no exceptions) to either enthusiastically get in the boat and start rowing, or be thrown overboard. As the late David Packard (Hewlett's partner) pointed out, "There can be no place for half-hearted interest or effort. ... A high degree of enthusiasm should be encouraged at all levels; in particular, the people in high management positions must not only be enthusiastic themselves, but they must be able to engender enthusiasm among their associates."[8] Failure to adhere to this "iron law" will wreak havoc within and inevitably doom any organization.

> *If you can't convey that message, graphically and credibly, with the very same crayon (literally), then you can't explain it, and your people ought not (and probably won't) invest in it!*

## 3. HOW DO WE PLAN TO GET THERE?

We believe that the *process* an organization uses to determine its destination is far less important than the methods used to communicate it and the level of discipline employed to get and keep people moving in the same direction. After the destination becomes clear, people have a right to know how you intend to get there. What's the game plan for achieving your destination? It's not that the entire plan needs to be laid out (in fact you are probably better off if there's a little room for improvisation), but the first two or three steps would be a great start.

### PLAYSCRIPTING

The wisdom of this approach was made apparent by former San Francisco 49ers head coach Bill Walsh. Over the course of his illustrious career, Walsh developed a practice he called "play scripting." On the day before a game, Walsh would simply make a list of the first 10 or 12 offensive plays his team would run the next day, and then share that list with his players in their Saturday night meeting. The result? According to Walsh, "The players liked it. They felt it eliminated some pregame anxiety, because they knew ahead of time what they would be doing on the first series. They had a chance to think about it, and most of them said they even slept better."[9] In 10 seasons under Walsh, the 49ers won three Superbowls and six NFL Western Division titles. Playscripting is now an indispensable part of game preparation for offensive coordinators throughout the NFL.

## 4. HOW DO I FIT IN?

Finally, people need to know what role you want them to play, and what it is you'll be expecting of them. Earlier we made the point that you've got to get the *big picture* indelibly burned into your employees' gray matter. You do. But people don't work day-to-day in the big picture. Instead, the proof is in the details, which, individually and taken together, send powerful messages that either confirm and lend support to, or contradict the big picture.

As organizations get larger, it's inevitable that people will begin to lose sight of where they fit in and how their contributions matter. Without regular and vigorous reinforcement on this point, people ultimately conclude that their contributions really do not matter all that much, and the decline in their effort is at hand. People who have come to believe that their role isn't all that important stand idly by and watch poor quality stuff go down the line; or a disgruntled customer go out the door; and they definitely don't hustle. Remember what Jim Barksdale said? "Motivated people move faster."

> *As organizations get larger, it's virtually inevitable that people will begin to lose sight of where they fit in and how their contributions matter.*

We *all* want to be a part of something important, and we want to play a meaningful role. Imagine for a moment how difficult it would be for *you* to remain Committed to something if you were the least bit uncertain about whether or not your efforts really mattered. We're often reminded of this point whenever there's a snowstorm of any size in our nation's capital, and the airwaves are immediately filled with announcements for government employees that "only people in essential positions need report for work." Now, deep down, who the hell wants something they spend eight hours a day doing to be deemed nonessential?

The moment your people feel that it's no longer important for them to do their very best work, your company has started down a very steep and slippery slope. Sorry for the replay, but the point bears repeating: "High expectations breed high performance."

*An individual without information cannot take responsibility. An individual who is given information cannot help but take responsibility.*[10]
—Jan Carlzon

## CHAPTER SUMMARY

1. Commitment starts with the *big picture*
   - What is this company all about?
   - Where are we going, and why?
   - How do we plan to get there?
   - How do I fit in?

2. You've got to be able to articulate it simply and credibly. Remember the crayons!

# SECTION THREE

## CONTENTED COWS ARE CARED ABOUT

# FIRST YOU FEED THE TROOPS

*The best and most successful commanders ... are those who win the respect, confidence, and affection of their subordinates by justice and firmness, tempered by kindness.*

—General John Schofield

It was a bleak and windy night on the remote island of Orkney—off the northern coast of Scotland—during World War II. Sergeant Major Jim Prentice of the Gordon Highlanders, a Scottish regiment of the British Army, was leading his men on maneuvers in preparation for the battles in Burma soon to come. Darkness had descended before four o'clock that afternoon, and now snow was falling at ten. The men were too far from their camp to get back without danger of freezing, so they were more than relieved to see the dim lights of a farm oasis not far ahead. They hoped the inhabitants would extend the hospitality of their barn for the war effort.

Sergeant Major Prentice knocked on the door of the farmhouse and awakened the farmer from his warm bed on that cold night. When he asked only if his men could sleep in the barn, the man patriotically gave his consent, but on the stipulation that all 30 of them first have a hot meal in his kitchen. The farmer roused his wife and kids from their sleep and the family prepared an inelegant feast of ground beef, potatoes, turnips, carrots, and pancakes. Six at a time, the soldiers warmed themselves and filled their insides in the farmer's tiny kitchen, while the others waited appreciatively in the barn.

The farmer's 9-year-old son watched curiously as Prentice, obviously the ranking soldier among them, ushered each group into the house. Only when all the troops had been served did he take a place at the table and eat. Curious at this unexpected behavior, the boy, who had been invited by the sergeant major to join him at the rough-hewn table, asked, "Why'd you go last? You're the leader!"

Prentice looked the young man in the eye and said with both conviction and instruction, "First you feed the troops. They're no good to you hungry."

More than 40 years went by before Prentice returned to that island at the edge of his own country. This time he came not as a soldier, but as a tourist, with his wife and grown daughter at his side. While his family toured the remains of a 5,000-year-old burial mound, he took a walk—a "wee donner" as he called it—up the road, as was his custom.

Prentice had not gone more than a few yards before he stumbled onto ground that bore a strange air of familiarity. As he wandered up to the house in the middle of the vast property, a man in his early fifties approached him. "Is there something I can help you with, sir?" Prentice explained the aura he sensed and began to ask the man questions about the farm. Then because the man seemed interested, he related to him the story of that night in 1940 when the kind farmer had taken in his troops and not only let them sleep in the barn, but …"First you feed the troops!" the man interrupted, shaking a knowing finger at the wizened face he now recognized.

"You're not the wee boy!" exclaimed Prentice.

"None other," said the farmer, and then he proceeded to bring his old friend up to date on the farm which he had inherited from his parents. His business had grown nearly fourfold in four decades! Until this conversation, Prentice had given no thought to the influence his simple act and single remark might have had on the young boy. Yet less than 10 years after the soldiers stopped by on that snowy evening, he had begun to take over the daily management of the farm. "I've always remembered what that sergeant major told me at the table," the farmer reminisced, "and even when the harvest was slim, and it was mighty slim some years, I've always made sure the hands working the farm had what they needed. You know, they're no good to you hungry."

## HUNGRY TROOPS: A COMPARATIVE STUDY IN WAR AND PEACE

In its 1991 coverage of the first and only four days of the ground phase of the Gulf War, CNN showed countless clips of bedraggled Iraqi soldiers emerging—hands high in the air—from their desert encampments and surrendering to U.S.-led coalition forces. What CNN did not show were the commanding officers of those troops. Not because CNN goofed, but because the officers, the so-called leaders of those troops, were not to be found. They were gone! Rather than stick it out with their men and risk an almost certain fate, they had vanished into the night.

Closer to home, but in roughly the same time frame, Texas businessman Ross Perot was leveling one blistering attack after another on the management of a major U.S. corporation. The corporation was General Motors, about which one can presume Perot knew more than most. On the heels of yet another "bad year," GM had served up huge bonus payouts to top managers, while at the same time failing to contribute the first nickel to the company's profit sharing plans. Hardly one to be anti-business or anti-bonus, Perot's point was simply that, "First you feed the troops. ..." Where have we heard that before?

While it would be both foolish and terribly unjust to paint the officers of GM and the Iraqi military with the same brush, they nonetheless were guilty of some of the same mistakes, and the larger organizations of which they were a part suffered as a result. In short, neither cared. In the case of GM, they didn't care about their people, who, in turn, cared less about the products they were making and the droves of customers who had stopped buying those products because they weren't very good.

## CARING CAN'T BE FAKED

First, let's establish the fact that caring is not a program, a technique, or something that can be taught or bought. It's not a *quid pro quo*. Caring is not about coddling people, making them feel comfortable, or providing false hope or security.

Your employees are a lot more rational than they are given credit for. They really don't expect a "free ride." They know, for example that you can't insulate them from anxiety and job stress any more than their homeowner's policy can keep a hurricane from roaring through their neighborhood. They also know that you really can't always guarantee the security of their jobs. Yet they still expect you to be fiercely Committed to things like being scrupulously honest with them, believing in them, helping them succeed, and being there for them when they need it. Rightly so. They know that when push comes to shove, you either care or you don't, and that nobody is a good enough actor or actress to fake it for long.

According to Tommy Lasorda, former manager of the Los Angeles Dodgers, the wise manager goes out of his or her way on a regular basis to let people know how important they are. "I want my players to know that I appreciate what they do for me. I want them to know that I depend on them. When you, as a leader of people, are naive enough to think that you, not your players, won the game, then you're in bad shape."[1] No doubt, that's one of the reasons Lasorda was frequently the first one out of the dugout to congratulate his players for making a big play.

As former America West CEO Mike Conway put it, "It's not that complicated. First you've got to care, and then you've got to demonstrate that you care by your actions because there is a natural skepticism out there. It's just not that complicated, but you've got to be committed to caring."[2]

### AMERICA WEST AIRLINES

|                                | 1995       | 1996       |
|--------------------------------|------------|------------|
| NUMBER OF AIRCRAFT             | 93         | 101        |
| AVAILABLE SEAT MILES (000)     | 19,421,451 | 21,624,529 |
| REVENUE PASSENGER MILES (000)  | 13,312,742 | 15,321,422 |
| PASSENGER ENPLANEMENTS         | 13,504     | 14,699     |

Source: America West PR Newswire, 1997.

In July of 1996, we met Angela Perry, a seven-year Delta flight attendant, who echoed the exact same sentiment but from an employee's perspective: "It all comes down to whether or not we believe that our management cares. If they do, we'll bend over backwards to look out for the company and our customers. If not, well ..."3

> *I feel that you have to be with your employees through all their difficulties, that you have to be interested in them personally. I want them to know that Southwest will always be there for them.*
> —Herb Kelleher, Southwest Airlines CEO

Caring is not a "photo-op." Rather, it's an attitude that's reflected by personal and organizational priorities. Organizations that care about their people take pains to ensure that human considerations are in the forefront of their decision making process when they develop corporate programs and policies, for example; or while acquiring and designing facilities, equipment, and systems; or when scheduling and arranging work. This is not something they do some of the time, or most of the time, but *always*, even when it's unpopular or seemingly less profitable to do so.

Without a doubt, there are degrees of caring and associated degrees of personal sacrifice which reflect how much you care. Despite what you may think of his political escapades, Ross Perot, founder and former chairman of Electronic Data Systems (which he later sold to General Motors) has provided one of the most visible and courageous examples in recent times of a leader who cares about his troops. As chronicled in Ken Follett's book, *On Wings of Eagles*, in 1979, Perot insisted on participating personally in the daring and dangerous rescue of two EDS employees who were being held hostage in Iran. According to Perot, "I talked Paul [Chiapparone] and Bill [Gaylord] into going over there [Iran], and I'm going to get them out."4 He did, and in the process demonstrated one of the most basic tenets of caring:

You've got to let people know you care about them by your physical presence when they are dealing with adversity.

> *Sincerity is the most important part of positive treatment. The only thing worse than a coach or CEO who doesn't care about his people is one who pretends to care. People can spot a phony every time. They know he doesn't care about them, and worse, his act insults their intelligence.*
>
> —Jimmy Johnson

## THE CUSTOMER COMES SECOND

Rosenbluth Travel CEO Hal Rosenbluth has done what some might consider going way out on a limb by titling his book *The Customer Comes Second*. He means *after* his employees. Southwest's Herb Kelleher says the same goes for his organization. Reportedly, he has invited more than one Southwest customer to find another airline when they became a bit too pushy or abusive with his people. These examples are not meant to suggest that "caring" organizations are at all cavalier about making money. On the contrary, they just happen to believe that doing right by their people will inevitably find its way to the bottom line—a much healthier bottom line, in fact. As evidenced by the following chart, which reflects the number of complaints filed per 100,000 passengers, Southwest customers apparently aren't too put out with them. (see Figure 5.1)

An organization's degree of caring is evidenced not by what it says but by what it does. (After all, what company in its right right mind would claim not to care?)

Since its inception, FedEx has espoused a rather simple business philosophy known as P–S–P (for People-Service-Profit). The fact that the "People" part comes first is no accident. The company attempts to demonstrate their philosophy in a host of ways, personnel decisions being one of them. As one might expect in such a high performance organization, performance standards

**FIGURE 5.1**

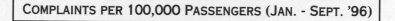

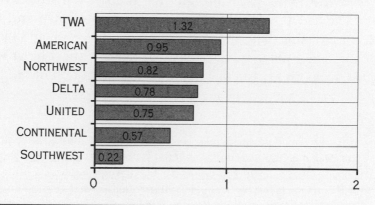

COMPLAINTS PER 100,000 PASSENGERS (JAN. - SEPT. '96)

| | |
|---|---|
| TWA | 1.32 |
| AMERICAN | 0.95 |
| NORTHWEST | 0.82 |
| DELTA | 0.78 |
| UNITED | 0.75 |
| CONTINENTAL | 0.57 |
| SOUTHWEST | 0.22 |

Source: U.S. Dept. of Transportation

and expectations are quite high, and not everyone measures up. But the quickest ticket out of that organization goes not to someone who has blown their budget or even disappointed a customer, but to anyone—especially a manager—who is disrespectful of or abusive toward another human being.

Let's go back to lunch at Renee's Sandwich Store. One of the reasons we think she has kept the same folks making her "Incredible Roast Beef Creations" and frying frozen potatoes for so long is that she cares about those often nameless faces who feed the masses each day. "These are the people who are making me money!" she shrieks as though it should be obvious, and she's right. Renee lends her employees money when they are in a pinch (which isn't often), and not one has ever abused her kindness. They all have their evenings free, so at least three times a year she takes the crew out to dinner. She gives them paid vacation—in a sandwich shop! And during the Christmas season, she puts up a little tree—like a special holiday tip jar—to which many appreciative customers paper clip "gifts." Who says money can't grow on trees?

"I care about them, and they care about me, and about each other. It's great," says this strong businesswoman with a personality that doesn't suffer slackers lightly. She once offered an employee the extra bedroom in her house, rent-free. Why? Because she had a social obligation to take in the down-and-out? No, Renee explains that "she was a damn good worker, and I knew that if she had a place to stay that was nearby, she'd be at work everyday. I was right, and she made us both a bunch of money."

> *A leader should possess human understanding and consideration for others. Men are not robots and should not be treated as such. I do not by any means suggest coddling. But men are intelligent, complicated beings who will respond favorably to human understanding and consideration. By these means their leader will get maximum effort from each of them. He will also get loyalty.*
>
> —General Omar Bradley

## GM: WHAT WENT WRONG?

Let's take time out right now to debunk a fairly popular myth. Caring about your people does not equate to lavishing them with money and expensive benefits, increases and extras which they haven't earned, the market doesn't require, and you can't afford. General Motors has been guilty of all three in its frequent capitulations to the United Auto Workers. Absent good and compelling reasons for these actions, GM has done itself and its employees (not to mention customers and shareholders) a huge disservice. Everyone involved knows it, too. Not unlike a "one night stand"; it may have felt good at the time, but they've been paying for it ever since.

One need only look at what has happened to GM's share of the U.S. car market and to their market value to know that something went seriously wrong. Between 1978 and 1995, for example, their share of the U.S. car and truck market slid from 46 to 32 percent.[5]

**FIGURE 5.2**

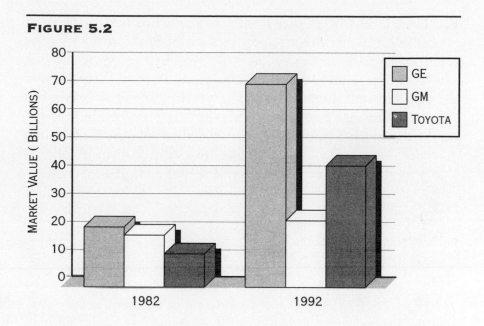

During the '80s and early '90s, when other industrial giants such as General Electric and Toyota saw their market value leap in excess of 20 percent annually, GM's managed barely a 5 percent annual gain.[6] (see Figure 5.2)

*People don't care how much you know until they know how much you care.*
—Anonymous

By providing benefits such as fully funded, zero-deductible health, vision, and dental care; supplemental unemployment insurance; and the like, by early 1996, GM had ratcheted its production labor costs into the $40-per-hour vicinity. This unfortunate development gave competitors such as parts maker Bosch an immediate cost advantage of roughly $20 per hour. Now, you've got to be pretty damned good to give your competitors a $20-an-hour head start and still expect to beat them in the marketplace. It would seem that when the cost of benefits started exceeding the cost of the steel needed to make cars, someone might have deduced that something was terribly amiss.

Instead, faced with losing roughly one-third of their U.S. car market share, continuing quality problems, an ocean of red ink ($23.5 billion in 1992 alone), and the loss of a sizable hunk of their stockholders' equity,[7] GM behaved just like the slow-boiled laboratory frog—the only difference being that the hand controlling the burner was their own! Asked by *Fortune* to explain what went wrong, then-GM boss Roger Smith was quoted as saying, "I don't know. It's a mysterious thing."[8]

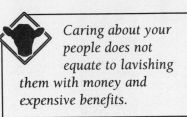

*Caring about your people does not equate to lavishing them with money and expensive benefits.*

Though admittedly a matter of opinion, we happen to believe that the problems at GM had far more to do with the attitudes and commitment level of its workforce (demoralized by an inattentive and uncaring management and a fractious relationship with the UAW) than with engineering, design, marketing, finance, or manufacturing processes. Think about it: GM enjoyed a huge brand name advantage; employed some of the best designers and marketing minds on the planet; had spent enough of their capital reserves on technological improvement to have bought Toyota outright; and yet they were still making crummy cars! Go figure.

Commenting on the company's partial recovery since the dark days of the late '80s and early '90s, Vice Chairman Harry B. Pearce said, "It is more than morale; it is a real feeling that people can make a difference. As big as this company is, you can always worry about people feeling they can have any impact. ..."[9] Indeed, Pearce's cause for concern had been effectively confirmed a couple of years earlier by Mark McKinney, one of his own production workers, who said, "To General Motors, you're a number. You're number 7795. This department needs a body, that department needs a body. ..."[10] People who feel they are nothing but a number or a body simply will not part with much of their discretionary effort.

Just who benefits when GM is forced to close a plant and Bosch or someone else gets all the business? In our view, two of the most uncaring things you can do to people are: (1) to give them something—whether they've earned it or not—knowing full well you'll have to ask for it back, and (2) to blow smoke up their noses (or other bodily orifices). How do you think your people see it?

## MOTIVATION DOESN'T NECESSARILY FOLLOW MONEY

We submit that inordinately high wages, salaries, and unwarranted benefits not only aren't the answer, they are often a large part of the problem. Moreover, they are often used as a counterbalance or way of compensating for serious deficiencies elsewhere in the organization. Of course, an organization cannot expect to maintain esprit de corps by paying substandard salaries, but a lot of damage (and not just to the current balance sheet) can be done when people see money being thrown around. Once this occurs, pay loses its meaning. Translation: The money must have been easily obtained. They know they're not worth that much. Remuneration loses its relevance and impact, like a Christmas morning when all the presents under the tree have your name on them.

> *Money will not necessarily buy you a peak performing organization.*

Money will not necessarily buy you a peak performing organization, either. The New York Yankees of the '80s and early '90s are perhaps a perfect example. With some of the most talent-laden rosters ever assembled on a baseball diamond (Winfield, Mattingly, Sax, et al.) and league-high payrolls, Yankee owner George Steinbrenner couldn't buy anything close to a championship. However, he did have some of those same big name players practically begging to be traded. Hmmm.

At the conclusion of the 1983 NFL season, the *St. Petersburg Times* (FL) published a study of the correlation between pay and performance for all the NFL football franchises (only 28 teams back then). Not unlike George Steinbrenner's experience, the results showed the following:

- The highest paid team in the NFL finished last.
- The lowest paid team won its division.
- The upper salary quartile produced no division winners.
- Two of the eight lowest paid teams won their division.
- Only one team in the upper salary quadrant won better than 50 percent of its games.
- The three highest paid teams finished last, next to last, and 21st.

We doubt seriously that the situation has changed much over the intervening years. In fact, we recall the 1995 Miami Dolphins and the 1996 New York Jets, both highly paid, underachieving teams loaded with expensive free-agents. True to form, the Jets had the worst record in football.

## WHEN TOO MUCH WORK IS NOT ENOUGH

Launching on average a new product every month in order to maintain their lead in the field of Internet access software, the employees of Netscape work incredibly long hours. Among the company's highly motivated engineers, 70-hour weeks are reportedly the norm, with round-the-clock stints common when it gets down to crunch time. The hours have become so crazy at times that the company has actually resorted to forcing people not to come to work. (How would you like to have that problem?)

### NETSCAPE COMMUNICATIONS CORPORATION

SELECTED FIRST QUARTER (JAN-MAR) FINANCIAL DATA,
IN $THOUSANDS, EXCEPT NET INCOME PER SHARE

|                       | 1996   | 1997    |
|-----------------------|--------|---------|
| REVENUES              | 56,121 | 120,241 |
| GROSS PROFIT          | 47,627 | 104,423 |
| NET INCOME            | 3,589  | 7,944   |
| NET INCOME PER SHARE  | $0.04  | $0.09   |

*Source:* Netscape First Quarter Financial Summary, 1997.

To give their people an edge and enable them to be more comfortable (and productive) when they are at work, Netscape employees generally set their own hours, dress the way they want, and furnish their workspace just like they would their home. While some have added sofas, refrigerators, stereos, and the like, Lou Montulli, a 23-year-old Netscape engineer, has furnished his cubicle with two huge aquariums.

You may be thinking about now that this whole idea sounds fishy, and Netscape is just another high tech California company destined for a train wreck because there's no sense of discipline and the "inmates are being allowed to run the asylum." Yet, surprisingly, these also happen to be some of the same practices employed by Southwest Airlines and Hewlett-Packard for nearly 30 years.

> *The only people who work this hard are people who want to.*
> —Jon Mittelhauser – a Netscape founding engineer

## YOUR PEOPLE ARE YOUR BEST COUNSEL, SO LISTEN!

Good leaders are smart enough to realize that the average employee is not likely to be completely candid with a "superior" in a strictly formal setting. Therefore, it becomes necessary from time to time to alter the manager/employee relationship in a controlled, constructive manner designed to remove all impediments to true communication. *Contented Cow* companies like Southwest Airlines, Federal Express, Rosenbluth Travel, and Disney—all detailed in the following examples—have perfected simple yet innovative methods for connecting with their workforce.

> *There's not any idea you can have [here] that people are not willing to listen to at any level. They want to help you develop it, and they'll go to any length to help you in any way they can.*
> —Soni Tron, production worker, North American Honda

## SOUTHWEST AIRLINES

One of the methods employed by Southwest to keep its management staff firmly grounded in the real world, while demonstrating that they care about their people, is a program requiring top managers to regularly spend time (at least one day per quarter) working alongside their people in the field. The executives handle baggage, answer reservation lines, and other important operating-level tasks. (Thankfully, this program excludes flying and aircraft maintenance duties!)

## FEDERAL EXPRESS

Like many other companies, FedEx performs an annual employee survey. But unlike other companies, they don't just ask the questions, tabulate the results, and then go back to sleep. They actually do something about those results. In other words, FedEx makes a serious effort to listen to their people through the survey results. How serious? For instance, the scores registered on the company's employee opinion survey (or SFA, for Survey-Feedback-Action) are a heavy factor in promotional decisions for managers. In fact, executive bonuses are paid only after a performance hurdle is cleared in each of three areas: Profitability, Customer Service, and—you guessed it—the Employee Opinion Survey Scores. In other words, the company could make a jillion dollars of net profit in a given year, but if their customers and employees aren't as satisfied as the shareholders, no executive bonuses.

> *We've all heard the criticism "he talks too much." When was the last time you heard someone criticized for listening too much?*
> —Norm Augustine

## ROSENBLUTH TRAVEL

Rosenbluth Travel CEO Hal Rosenbluth conducts the surveys and a whole lot more. In addition to having a special hot-line for employees to contact him directly with suggestions or criticism,

Rosenbluth spends two days a year working with and listening to randomly selected associates. Moreover, he makes sure the company's 360-degree review program starts with him, and sponsors an "Associate of the Day" program in which any of the company's 3,000 employees has the opportunity to spend a day working alongside him or another senior executive of their choice.

## DISNEY

Introducing an average of 80 to 90 new products each year, fresh ideas are absolutely crucial to a company like Disney. They recognize the need to listen and are enthusiastic about creating opportunities to hear their employees. In a 1996 speech before the Chicago Executives Club, CEO Michael Eisner detailed a playful but effective process his company uses to solicit ideas from its people. Several times each year,

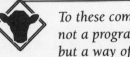

*To these companies it's not a program at all, but a way of life!*

various Disney divisions host their own version of TV's once popular "Gong Show." Employees are encouraged to bring forward their product ideas for consideration by the company's top brass. According to Eisner, "Anybody who wants to, and I mean anybody, gets a chance to pitch an idea for an animated film to a small group of executives, which includes, among others, me and Roy Disney, our vice chairman, and Peter Schneider, head of Feature Animation. For this to work, you must have an environment where people feel safe about giving their ideas. … Yes, we gong people if we think an idea won't work, but we tell them why and we tell them how it might be improved."[11]

Clearly, the above mentioned efforts aren't rocket science—they never are—but you've got to believe that GM's Roger Smith might have had a better idea about what was wrong with his company had some comparable plan or program been in existence there. For companies like Disney and FedEx, however, you get the sense the plan or program is relatively unimportant in the overall scheme of things. In fact, to these companies it's not a program at all, but a way of life! What matters most is that this ultra-simple approach is backed up by diligent action, day after day after day. As Southwest's Vice President for People Libby Sartain puts it, "I keep telling them [her HR peers] that it's all about values and caring and treating people like you want to be treated and their eyes glaze over. They want the quick answer."[12]

> *The leader must have time to listen to his men. It is easy to look important and say, 'I haven't got time,' but each time the leader does it, he drives one more nail in the coffin of the team spirit whose life he should really be cherishing.*
> —Lincoln Andrews, a West Point faculty member under MacArthur

## CHAPTER SUMMARY

1. Caring is an attitude, not a program. It has nothing whatsoever to do with sentiment, emotions, or "being nice."

2. First, you feed the troops.

3. Motivation doesn't necessarily follow money.

4. If you care about your people, you listen to them, really listen!

**Best Practices:**

1. Southwest Airlines' executive day at the operating level.
2. FedEx's Survey-Feedback-Action.
3. Rosenbluth Travel's employee day at the management level.
4. Disney's "Gong Show."

# 6

# TELL 'EM
# THE TRUTH

*We adopted a philosophy that we wouldn't hide anything, not any of our problems, from the employees.*
—Rollin King, founder of Southwest Airlines

## TRUTH OR CONSEQUENCES

Few things abound within the employment arena more poisonous than insincerities, half-truths, insidious omissions, and just plain lies. One of the principal reasons the truly great companies find themselves atop the summit of success year after year is because they go to great lengths to avoid confusing people by lying to them, most particularly, those people who are or aspire to be on their payroll. They don't lay out a bunch of Dilbert-type platitudes which they either can't or don't intend to live up to and, at the same time, they are very plainspoken and unapologetic about things they do feel strongly about.

If you care about your people, you make it a point to tell them the truth, even when (and especially when) it hurts. Good leaders make it a point to deliver bad news in an up-close-and-personal way. As Dennis LeStrange of IKON Office Solutions puts it, "People need to hear the bad news directly, from the person who made that decision, rather than read it in a memo; and they deserve to hear it early."[1]

Seeking to avoid the shackles imposed by unionism and our judicial system over the past decades, American industry—largely at the urging of human resource practitioners and labor attorneys—has adopted an overly conservative (some might call it mealy mouthed) approach to dealing with employee performance issues. The atmosphere of caution is so pervasive, in fact, that in the course of tip-toeing around possible charges of discrimination, favoritism, wrongful discharge, and the like, managers have in many cases completely lost sight of the mission at hand, namely fixing performance errors! And yet we wonder why it's so difficult to improve things like quality and productivity, and why people get so upset with us when we finally do tell them there's a problem with their performance.

## MALICE IN WONDERLAND

In the 1980s, we did some work for a company we'll refer to as Giant. With nearly two billion dollars in annual revenues and an employee population near 40,000, the company was sizable indeed. However, because they were finding it necessary to terminate the services of a high number of employees for performance-related reasons, Giant's management determined that they had a problem. In one 18-month span, for example, they terminated some 986 people, not for egregious transgressions like lying, cheating, or stealing, but for doing a crummy job. Tasked by the CEO with looking into this and coming up with some answers, we began investigating the situation. We searched in all the usual places and talked to all the usual suspects—some of the "firees" as well as the managers who had done the dastardly deeds. We combed through personnel files, examined hiring practices, and did a massive search through Giant's rather sophisticated HR information system.

At some point, we learned of Giant's "Performance Review Policy," which was pretty standard, requiring formal written reviews every six months until death or termination. A staff member hammered his way through the HR system, trying to find a correlation between poor reviews and the terminations, but quickly returned with the news that there was "obviously a flaw in either the data itself or the search parameters, as no correlation could be found."

Wait a minute! We asked him to take another look at the data. At the same time, we had someone physically look at the review forms contained in the hard copy records. In the end, the conclusion was the same: There was no correlation between the reviews and the terminations. Giant managers had dutifully conducted performance reviews with every one of these 986 people in the six months immediately preceding their termination, but in only three of those cases had they actually informed the employee that they were doing an unsatisfactory job! *Incredibly, roughly two-thirds of these same people had also received merit increases in the six months preceding their termination!* We submit that, sad as it is, what was happening at Giant is more the rule than the exception. In fact, it's probably going on right now in your company. Go find out!

Now, we are not suggesting that the whole world gets up in the morning and says, "I think I'll go to work and tell a fib today." Lying is not that deliberate or direct, yet too often it seems second nature in workplace situations, just like at Giant. To be honest, it starts before the person is even hired.

## LIAR, LIAR

Most managers walk around with the well-founded suspicion that people are going to lie to them in the employment interview process. Many do, to be sure. But how frequently do they receive the same in kind before the interview is even half way through. Sound familiar?

Applicant:     "So what's it like working around here?"

Manager:     [preoccupied with getting the wash out, the cars built, burgers flipped, etc.] "It's a great place to work. ... It's almost like family."

[Yeah, the dysfunctional sort.]

Applicant:     "How will I learn the job?"

Manager:     "Oh, we've got an extensive orientation and training program."

[Right, it probably lasts all morning.]

Applicant:     "What are the big bosses like?"

Manager:     "They're great people. They really believe in putting people first. Just look here in our annual report at what our Chairman and CEO said, 'I am confident because I am so proud of the job being done by our more than 300,000 people.'"

[Was that before or after all the layoffs, buyout offers, and your big raise?]

But that exchange seems innocent compared to what happens once they come on board. In his book, *The Dilbert Principle,* master satirist Scott Adams has categorized what he terms the "Great Lies of Management." In a fashion similar to that employed by a popular late night TV show, here they are:

#13. Your input is important to us.

#12. Our people are the best.

#11. We'll review your performance in six months.

#10. I haven't heard any rumors.

#9. Training is a high priority.

#8. We don't shoot the messenger.

#7. Performance will be rewarded.

#6. We reward risk takers.

#5. The future is bright.

#4. We're reorganizing to better serve our customers.

#3. You could earn more money under the new plan.

#2. I have an open door policy.

and the #1 all-time great lie:

drum roll, please

#1. Employees are our most valuable asset.[2]

The principle of "truth or consequences" is certainly simple enough. Yet it is violated on a regular basis as companies spew forth one philosophy while practicing quite another. The only thing we're suggesting is that, especially when it comes to communicating with your workforce, PR should take a distant back seat to honesty. If your company is a tough place to work, say so, and be very explicit in explaining why and how. Don't apologize for it! If your business is in trouble, say so. And for pete's

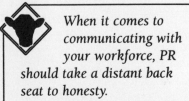

*When it comes to communicating with your workforce, PR should take a distant back seat to honesty.*

sake, if an employee is screwing up, say so; that's what managers get paid for. So, either step up to the plate or go sit in the dugout!

*I didn't lie to anyone.*
   —Don Shula, when asked what he'd like to be remembered for

## CHAPTER SUMMARY

If you care about your people, you tell them the truth, period.

1. People need to hear the bad news directly from the person who made that decision, rather than read it in a memo; and they deserve to hear it early.

2. The whole problem with Performance Reviews is not the form, the frequency, or the lack of rater objectivity, but a lack of honesty!

3. Just like at home where we teach our children to lie at an early age ("Tell 'em Daddy's not here."), we begin early at work, before people are even on our payroll!

Worst Practice: Giant's "Performance Review Policy" (and probably yours).

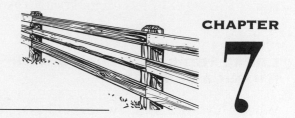

# WHEN TIMES
# GET TOUGH

*He'll sit there and listen. I mean, really listen. He's in our corner. That takes the load off. Then when you go on the football field and the man says, 'Look, I want you to run down there, catch that ball and run into that wall,' then who are you to say 'no'? You catch that ball and you run into that wall. You say, 'Okay, Coach, you were there for me; now I'm gonna give it up for you.' That's crucial.*
—Michael Irvin, Dallas Cowboy wide receiver, talking about his former coach, Jimmy Johnson

## IF YOU CARE, YOU'RE THERE

Perhaps more than anything else they can do, organizations and their leaders demonstrate that they care by their physical presence when times are tough. In our view, there is something of a quid pro quo involved here. Recall from the first chapter that by definition, discretionary effort is a contribution people can make if they want, but only if they want. The inclination to part with some of that discretionary effort is based, at least in part, on the individual's perception of how things would go if the shoe were on the other foot. In other words, "You're asking me to walk through fire for you? Would you do the same for me? Have you done the same for me?"

## LOCAL HEROES: RYDER'S RESPONSE TO HURRICANE ANDREW

When Hurricane Andrew roared across South Florida in 1992, thousands of homes were destroyed and tens of thousands were left homeless, including many of Ryder's 2,000 employees in the Miami area. On an institutional level, as soon as the winds subsided, Ryder—the five billion dollar commercial truck leasing and logistics giant—began making on-the-spot, interest-free loans up to $10,000 to employees who needed it, and dispatching repair crews to the homes of employees (and their neighbors!) who had been hardest hit by the hurricane.[1]

On a personal level, Ryder Chairman, CEO and President Tony Burns (whose own home suffered severe damage as well) began spending as much time personally delivering needed supplies to employee homes and helping with repairs as he did tending to corporate business. Said Burns, "I really think being a good citizen and offering opportunity to all people is not only the absolute right thing to do, it's also great business. Customers want to do business with you, and employees want to work here."[2]

### RYDER SYSTEM, INC. NET INCOME FOR 1991–1995

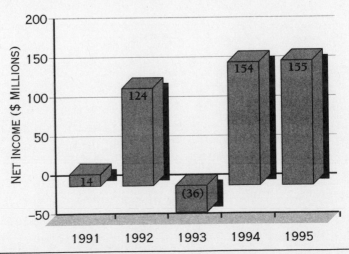

*Source:* Hoover Handbook of American Business

## IF YOU REBUILD IT, MORE WILL COME

On the night of December 11, 1995, in the tiny town of Lawrence, Massachusetts, residents were horrified as Malden Mills, one of the town's major employers (2,500-plus jobs), saw the lion's share of its textile manufacturing capacity burn to the ground. Undaunted, Aaron Feuerstein, the mill's 70-year-old owner, vowed that "with God's help, we will overcome the events of the past 12 hours and continue to be a vital force in New England." One of the first things Feuerstein did was give each employee a paycheck, a $275 Christmas bonus, a coupon redeemable for food at a local grocery store, and, more significantly, his personal assurance that their salaries and benefits would be protected for a minimum of one month (a time frame he subsequently extended not once but *twice* as the rebuilding process wore on).3

> *On an institutional and personal level "Contented Cow" companies tend to do a much better job of putting their bodies and their money where their mouths are.*

Malden Mills did rebuild, and their customers stuck with them. Now Feuerstein can't understand what all the commotion was about. "I simply did a normal thing," he said. If that's such a normal thing for a 70-year-old man, why shouldn't it be for the rest of us? While some might brand Feuerstein a saint for paying out $15 million in wages and benefits he wasn't required to pay, others may consider him a fool for not taking the insurance money and running—either to his own retirement, or at least to a lower cost area in which to rebuild.

Neither is the case. Feuerstein is an astute business person capable of making incredibly rational decisions even in the presence of a still-smoldering factory. First of all, factories are typically insured for their replacement value, and any insurance payoff would likely be limited to the depreciated value of the property had he chosen not to rebuild. Second, assuming the business earned Feuerstein $20 million on its $400 million or so in revenues, he and his family would be walking away from a lot of money over the course of two or three generations had they opted out. And finally, Feuerstein has got this *Contented Cow* thing absolutely, positively figured out. With both customer and employee retention rates already hovering around 95 percent (do you suppose there's any relationship?), imagine what new heights his business might reach with a new factory and the same highly skilled, well-trained, and now emotionally turbocharged people running it?

No matter their size, both on an institutional and personal level, *Contented Cow* companies tend to do a much better job of putting their bodies and their money where their mouths are.

About 10 months after the Malden Mills fire, a similar event took place in Memphis, Tennessee, when a vicious thunderstorm took the roof off a local eatery by the name of Fred Gang's. The owner, Jack Stout, responded just as Feuerstein had done. "We're maintaining any person who was on the payroll … at full wages, *including lost tip compensation*," said Stout. While his restaurant was closed upwards of three months, Stout did not flinch. "We've had people with us five, 10, 12 years, and some since the restaurant opened in 1976," he said. "Fred Gang's is more than a paycheck to them."[4]

> *People just want to know that somebody knows, and cares.*
> —Dennis P. LeStrange, IKON Office Solutions

## PROVIDE SOME SYSTEM OF JUSTICE

Caring must occur on a systemic as well as on a personal basis. People need to feel a sense of justice and know the answer to the dreaded but almost certain question: "Where do I go with a problem?" In the words of Alan Westin, Columbia University law professor, "Corporations must do justice well internally, or have it done for them."[5] We think it's inevitable that whenever a person has a complaint or concern, something is going to happen, whether it's sanctioned by the organization or not. In those cases where there is no sponsored mechanism—or one not working properly—people will resort to what might be termed "self-prescribed remedies." In short, they'll take matters into their own hands.

Certainly from the company's standpoint, the most dangerous option employees have is to fix the problem themselves. The least visible and perhaps most effective way of doing this is by simply "powering back" a notch or two. Whenever the employees' focus of attention shifts from productive effort to worrying about their problems, the result is the withholding of discretionary effort. It's nearly imperceptible, almost impossible to manage, and, not unlike Mr. Garfield's experience with the hungry Eastern flight attendants, invariably winds up in your customer's lap.

Before you dismiss this as something that happens only at failed organizations like Eastern, consider the results of a 1996 Gallup Poll which reported that fully 25 percent of us are angry at work. Not disappointed or disillusioned—angry! Younger workers (ages 18–34) are madder than older folks (the over 50 crowd). Hendrie Weisinger, a Westport, Connecticut, psychologist offers a list, in no particular order, of what gets the American worker hot under the proverbial collar, be it of the white or blue variety:

1. harassment, sexual or otherwise
2. favoritism of one employee over another
3. insensitivity of managers
4. depersonalization of the workplace, causing employees to feel as if they're just numbers
5. unfair performance appraisals
6. lack of resources, including everything from support staff to corporate credit cards
7. lack of adequate training
8. lack of teamwork
9. withdrawal of earned benefits
10. lack or violation of trust
11. poor communication
12. absentee bosses

If you would like to see further proof, pay a quick visit to *http://www.disgruntled.com*, an internet Web site created specifically for people to vent their spleen about perceived injustices in their workplace. The fact that the site exists isn't in and of itself particularly remarkable. After all, there's a Web site for just about everything. But what *is* a little unsettling is the sheer volume of published complaints, and the inescapable fact that most of them are being penned from the workplace. (In fact, software publisher Daniel Levine has incorporated a "Boss Escape" icon which enables users to quickly shift to a screen image which more closely resembles the work they're being paid to do at the moment.) In a seemingly unending stream of letters signed: "In a Show Me State of Shock"; "Sick of the Hospital I Work In"; and "Hapless Sap," to name only a few, employees describe a plethora of vexations and troubles, many of which pertain in one way or another to the issue of job security.

While on the surface an aggrieved employee may appear to do nothing about the situation, the fact remains that people really don't forget about their perceived injustices. Rather, they file them away and accumulate others until a breaking point is reached. At which time, they escalate their demand for justice.

All too often, an employee who has moved on to a more overt plan of action will find someone else to help them with their problem. While the number of people turning to unions to accomplish this has been steadily declining for 20 years, don't count organized labor out, especially in view of moves like the AFL-CIO's decision to boost spending on organizing from $2.5 million in 1995 to $30 million in 1997.[6] Many Americans were reminded of this in August of 1997, when the Teamsters Union effectively shut down United Parcel Service for two weeks, and brought much of the commercial sector to a screeching halt.

## UNION MEMBERSHIP

| % OF ALL EMPLOYEES | YEAR | TOTAL MEMBERS (MILLIONS) |
|---|---|---|
| 18.0 | 1985 | 17.0 |
| 17.5 | 1986 | 16.9 |
| 17.0 | 1987 | 16.9 |
| 16.8 | 1988 | 17.0 |
| 16.4 | 1989 | 16.9 |
| 16.1 | 1990 | 16.7 |
| 16.1 | 1991 | 16.6 |
| 15.8 | 1992 | 16.4 |
| 15.8 | 1993 | 16.6 |
| 15.5 | 1994 | 16.7 |
| 14.9 | 1995 | 16.4 |
| 14.5 | 1996 | 16.3 |

*Source:* U.S. Bureau of Labor Statistics

Meanwhile, it has become increasingly popular for people to involve other outside advocates like agents, lawyers, and state or federal agencies to get what they want. According to the latest information from the American Bar Association, there are 966,000 lawyers alive and presumably very well in the United States (34,000 of them on federal payrolls alone). That's one for every 270 persons. If a 1996 finding by the U.S. Dept. of Labor is any indication, all those attorneys have been working overtime because, since 1991, the number of suits filed for unlawful discrimination and harassment has tripled!

*Stay away from the courthouse; you'll never make any money there.*
—J.E. Davis, founder of Winn-Dixie Stores

## FAST, FAIR AND ADMINISTRABLE JUSTICE

*Contented Cow* organizations realize that whenever you've got two or more people working in some common endeavor, there are going to be perceived injustices and serious problems which arise from time to time. They realize too that most people really don't want to sue their employer, join a labor union, or involve an outside agency, let alone quit their job. So, rather than waiting to be victimized by one or another of the self-prescribed remedies, they proactively install some system which tolerates and even encourages the airing and resolution of the problem, so people can get on with the business at hand.

In 1990, Dennis Spina took over the helm of one of the nation's largest propane distributors, Suburban Propane. Experiencing a decline in retail sales and margins due to eroding service and historically high prices, Suburban had nearly 8,000 extremely nervous employees, and customers defecting in droves.

Moreover, Suburban had recently acquired Petrolane, one of its largest competitors, in a heavily leveraged deal. With all these negatives conspiring against him, and in addition to being on the verge of a disastrous "heating season" (an extremely mild winter), Spina had his hands full. New to the propane business, Spina spent the bulk of his first 10 days riding with and working alongside the company's delivery drivers. That act itself should have sent a clear message to headquarters staffers and company officers, many of whom probably wouldn't have recognized one of their own delivery vehicles if it ran over them.

What came next was an even bigger shock. Spina assembled roughly a dozen of the company's "best and brightest," drawing equally from the managerial, professional, and hourly ranks. He told them essentially that there were still a lot of things about the business he didn't understand, and probably some things he never would. But one thing he did know was that the only way to resolve one of their very greatest concerns—notably for their future—was to sell more gas and find ways to deliver it more efficiently, to more satisfied customers. Continuing, he added, "And we'll never be able to do that as long as you have to spend even one minute of your precious time looking over your shoulder wondering and worrying about something bad happening to you because of the capricious act of a manager or, more probably, some unintentionally dumb corporate practice. The only thing I want you and your co-workers to worry about is doing your job the best way you know how."

Spina then instructed the group to create some sort of problem and complaint resolution mechanism that would serve as something of a safety net for Suburban employees. The only constraints he put on the project were that whatever they came up with had to be "fast, fair, and administrable." A few months later, the group emerged with an ultra-simple three-step process which they subsequently named EARS (Employee Appeal and Review System). In announcing its implementation, Spina said, "[EARS] will afford our employees the opportunity to have workplace disputes resolved in a fair, objective, and timely manner by the people who know them best. We must recognize that if an employee has a problem, then the company has a problem, and it's to everyone's advantage to get it resolved immediately, before it becomes a customer problem."

We believe EARS represents the cutting edge of corporate problem and complaint resolution procedures. After the installation of the EARS procedure, Spina commented to us, "One of the unintended benefits was that this process forced a level of introspection that made us look at some of those policies and procedures which placed our customer contact people in a position of having to explain dumb actions by the corporate bureaucracy."

## DON'T EXPECT EMPLOYEES TO PAY FOR YOUR MISTAKES

Companies demonstrate whether or not they care by the extent to which they expect their people to pay for managers' mistakes. Sometimes employees are asked to give up perks they once enjoyed, which isn't always a bad thing to do, especially in light of the alternatives. But people take an understandably dim view of the matter when that sacrifice is caused by (or occurs in the face of) managerial indiscretions or extravagances.

> *Companies demonstrate whether or not they care by the extent to which they expect their people to pay for managers' mistakes.*

Consider, for example, the case of a large southern hospital. When faced with the prospect of having to lay off more than 100 full-time employees, they decided instead on an ambitious cost-cutting program, which is detailed in the following excerpt from a memo distributed to all hospital staff:

(Our editorial comments appear in brackets [].)

**MEMORANDUM**

As part of our Continuous Quality Improvement process [please!], we must continually look for ways to improve efficiency. This is particularly true as we move deeper into a managed care [some would say mangled care] environment. One way to do that is to reduce expenses, which places us in a better position to bid on health care contracts. [So far, it sounds reasonable.] As we receive more contracts because of lower cost pricing, we will assist in increasing the probability of stable employment for the future. [Yeah, right. We'll have to wait and see about that.]

Effective [such-and-such date], the following "expense improvements" [write that one down] will be implemented:

- Hourly shifts will be cut from 13 to 12 hours and overtime will be eliminated, saving $1.2 million.
- The five holidays for which we now pay premium overtime will be reduced to three, saving $127,000.
- The weekend differential will be cut from 30 percent to $2/hour, saving $806,000.
- The number of compensated days off for salaried employees will be cut from 13 to eight, saving us $227,000.
- The tuition reimbursement plan will be eliminated, saving $1.2 million.

The total cost savings of the above will total more than $3.5 million, allowing us to stabilize employment for 107 full-time employees.

On the surface, the memo doesn't sound unreasonable at all. It's kind of the old "let's all pull together to keep this ship afloat" idea, one which we support. What the memo left out was the $4.1 million capital expenditure in the same year for such health-improving hospital features as a new marble entranceway, expanded lobby complete with a one-million-dollar aquarium and attendant staff, and new china for executive functions.

The grumbling over the cost cuts turned to loud shouts and defections when the opulence was installed. And then a year later, after all the selective belt-tightening, a hundred more people received "unstable employment"; they were laid off. All we can say is that we're glad neither of us lives near enough this hospital to depend on it for health care. We imagine there are some pretty discontented cows running around the place. And while we're sure they're all behaving professionally, we don't even want to think about the dangerous combination of a mad cow with a needle or proctoscope!

While the eventual layoffs at the hospital may seem cruelly handled and only halfheartedly forestalled, "guaranteed employment" is every bit as unjust and unkind. Inevitably, both the individual employee (whose performance is failing), and that person's co-workers (who must carry the extra load), will get swept out the door together when the grim reaper appears. Yet companies must not be deluded by false hopes or unrealistic expectations when scaling back their workforce.

*Sometimes a change of pasture will make the cow fatter.*
　　　　　　　　　　　　　　—American frontier saying

Above all else, companies should be very careful how much faith they put in the savings projected to occur via their downsizing, re-engineering, or—insert your own code word for "layoff"—efforts. Studies by the American Management Association and others have proven conclusively that most such efforts result in no near-term improvement in operating profits, or productivity. A survey of 531 large business organizations conducted by the Wyatt Company showed that, among companies that had undergone "restructuring," only 46 percent saw any attendant increase in earnings within two years following the restructuring. Less than 34 percent of those same companies realized an increase in productivity from the layoffs, and better than half of the companies actually refilled the positions they had eliminated within a year of downsizing![7] (And we wonder why some refer to the practice as "dumbsizing.")

> *I wasn't smart enough about that [speaking of the "People Factor"]. I was reflecting my engineering background and was insufficiently appreciative of the human dimension. I've learned that's critical.*[8]
> —Michael Hammer, the "Father of Re-engineering"

## CORPORATE INSANITY

While there's not much evidence to suggest that layoffs really help, they are a trend that doesn't seem to be going away. Challenger, Gray & Christmas, an outplacement firm that keeps tabs on such numbers, reported in July of 1996 that 312,356 corporate layoffs had been announced in the first half of that year, up 33 percent over the 1995 midyear tally.[9] As we see it, there are two opposing and equally important schools of thought on the subject.

First, as the frequency and pace of change in the commercial landscape increases, companies are propelled in and out of business sectors and markets at an ever-more-rapid rate. It seems an immutable fact that the days when employees could reasonably expect to have a one-company career if they so wished are pretty much over, perhaps forever. From now on, nearly all businesses will continue to find themselves reacting to an over or under supply of labor as they relentlessly pursue "better, faster, and cheaper."

No matter how great the hue and cry is over management's obsession with the short term outlook, market forces have spoken. In fact, given that nearly everyone these days has money in the market—via a 401(k) or IRA—a Cleveland pipe fitter is just as inclined as any Wall Street analyst to raise hell when earnings don't meet or exceed targets every quarter. In an interview not long ago, Peter Lynch, former manager of Fidelity's Magellan Fund, pretty much echoed this thought. "All of us are looking for the best deals in clothing, computers, and telephone service—and rewarding the high-quality, low-cost providers with our business," he observed. "I haven't met one person who would agree to pay AT&T twice the going rate for phone service if AT&T would promise to stop laying people off."[10]

*Worried cows don't make very productive (let alone, contented) cows.*

> *While at General Electric, I said at one time that we should be striving to have all our employees ready to go and anxious to stay. ... If workers feel their employer is keeping them employable at all times [via growth and learning], their sense of insecurity will diminish.*
> —Frank Doyle, chairman of the Committee for Economic
> Development, and retired executive
> vice president of General Electric

Second, from the opposite side of the fence, we think the extent to which employees are concerned about the prospect of *losing* their jobs mirrors inversely the extent to which they are concerned with *doing* their jobs. In short, worried cows don't make very productive (let alone, *contented*) cows. The folks you are counting on to deliver high quality goods or services to your customers mustn't be too busy worrying about their own futures to *care* (important word) about the business.

While layoffs are indeed at times a necessary event, there is a big difference between grudgingly accepting them as a final desperate act of corporate survival versus what Springfield Remanufacturing CEO Jack Stack calls "corporate insanity" (i.e., a convenient way to periodically trim a little fat). In either case, there's no getting around the fact that they are a sign of management failure. According to Stack, "You lay people off when you've screwed up, when you've guessed wrong about the market, when you haven't anticipated some critical development or created adequate contingency plans. It's a sign of how badly management has failed, and the people who get hurt are invariably those who had nothing to do with creating the problem in the first place."[11]

## SOME RULES FOR "STAYING OUT OF THE SOUP"

Here are some precepts we believe will help you avoid this unpleasantness altogether, if you'll only execute them faithfully:

1. Spend 10 times as much time worrying about the *quality* of employees being added to your payroll as you do the number of them. As Machiavelli said, "The first method for estimating the intelligence of a ruler is to look at the men he has around him."

2. Adopt outrageously high performance expectations, continually "raise the bar," and on an ongoing basis, reassign or remove people who don't measure up. As you're going about this, don't allow loyalty to be confused with competence. Do it humanely, but do it! Initiate a "career change" for managers who can't or won't do this.

3. Eliminate every single systemic inducement to adding unnecessary headcount. Never, for example, tie anyone's pay, position, or perks to the number of people they "supervise."

4. After doing the first three, be as judicious about adding head-count at work as you are at home.

5. Finally, don't allow profitability or "affordability" to cloud your judgment or lower your standards on any of the above, ever.

In the final analysis, how layoffs are perceived by your work-force (and the buying public) comes down to your corporate mind-set. If it's acceptable in your organization one day to hire people "full-time," and then send them home a few months or years later—simply because you've miscalculated your requirement for labor or ability to profitably sell a product or service—then you don't care.

Some organizations are characterized by a sort of binge-and-purge personality—"corporate bulimics," if you will—caught up in a capricious cycle of staffing up and laying off to meet labor demands exactly. We are not talking about hiring temps, or a strategic decision to permanently outsource certain non-core activities. Rather, we mean those companies which routinely hire and lay off because they erroneously think it's a good way to do business. Rarely if ever do they acknowledge the consequences of the emotional upheaval visited upon the employees involved—not only those who leave, but particularly the ones who stay—and its impact on the overall health of the organization.

To be fair, we know most CEOs agonize a great deal over the decision to send some people home so that the jobs of others might be preserved. Thoughtfully and regretfully, at times they must conclude that it is the only unfortunate course of action to take.

If you DO find yourself in the unenviable position of having to send people home, there are some things you can do to make it easier on all concerned:

1. Make sure that you've first exhausted all alternative remedies (shortened workweeks, voluntary pay reductions, job reassignments, and the like). In the same vein, people who have demonstrated themselves as non-performers should be dealt with as such, in advance of any workforce reduction.

2. Get it over with quickly and at once. While "sudden death" is bad enough, the lingering variety is unconscionable. In the words of "Chainsaw Al" Dunlap, "What I keep uppermost in my mind is that if I don't release them today, I'm going to have to cut more of them in six months or a year anyway. Doing it piecemeal is a fraud upon everybody—the employees, management, and the shareholders."[12]

3. Make sure the pain inflicted on top management occurs first, and is clearly disproportionate. In Perot-type terms, the officers must bleed first, and most; or, as "Chainsaw" puts it, "Start at the top! Get rid of the corporate toys, squeeze the corporate headquarters, shrink high-priced management. The last thing you do is deal with the unions, so they know you went after real waste first."[13]

4. Don't hide anything from anybody. Your rationale for making these moves needs to be painfully evident and unassailable. Failure to make this case will fuel understandable anger, and frustration, not to mention a permanent loss of trust.

5. When it's over, say so, and mean it. Turn your attention immediately to enacting serious measures that will help you make damn sure you don't have to go down this road again.

## ANHEUSER BUSCH

Not unlike others we're aware of, Anheuser Busch deserves credit for the way it has decided to regulate the numbers in its labor force. In January 1997, the nation's largest brewer, anticipating a need for a reduction in its workforce in the years to come, instituted a hiring freeze rather than layoffs. Like putting the company on a sensible diet, it is a far better response than the bingeing and purging to which the untreated corporate bulimic is doomed.

## RUBBERMAID

Lately, Wolfgang Schmitt, CEO of Rubbermaid, has found himself under pressure to do something about his company's slowing rate of growth. Says Schmitt, "Sure, we could take out a lot of our people. But we could give up our future. One, we'd demotivate the people who remained. Two, they surely wouldn't have the loyalty they now have. Three, if there were any good people left, they wouldn't be here long. They'd be looking around. And uncertainty reduces risk taking."[14] Remember, this isn't a moral argument, but rather, a quest for credibility that goes directly to the hearts and minds of the people on your payroll.

The *Contented Cow* companies have figured out you cannot have it both ways. Corporation by corporation and business unit by business unit, they have defined the sanctity of long term employment prospects, what conditions they were willing to accept, and baked them into the equation. For too long, leaders have ducked these responsibilities, preferring instead to try to play the game with two completely different sets of rules. Get on one side of the fence or the other. No one is asking you to make a moral judgment, only a very practical one. So, do it!

## ZAPMAIL

It is important to realize that disaster and extinction are not the same thing. FedEx proved this point in the mid-1980s when faced with the prospect of losing roughly half its business to electronic document transmission—the company launched its ill-fated ubiquitous fax service known as ZapMail. Not one to do things in a small way, FedEx spent over a billion dollars developing the technology, getting satellite transponder time, and hiring a dedicated workforce to sell, maintain, and deliver the service.

Despite some pretty sophisticated planning, what the company didn't count on was the space shuttle *Challenger* disaster, which severely constrained satellite transponder availability; the effects of the AT&T breakup on the ability to get dedicated land lines; and the sheer explosiveness of facsimile growth. These developments spelled the demise of ZapMail. When they finally pulled the plug on the project, FedEx found itself with a lot of expensive gear and about 1,300 people it absolutely, positively didn't need.

> *Disaster and extinction are not the same thing.*

Amid all the consternation associated with shutting down the service, one seemingly all-important subject—layoffs—was never even broached. Based on a commitment founder Fred Smith made to his employees years earlier, the company promised never to send anybody home unless the very survival of the whole enterprise was at stake. Every single member of the defunct Zap-Mail division was offered a job elsewhere in the company. In the end, some took the offer, and some didn't, but it was their choice. According to Smith, "We reorganized and absorbed virtually every person into the workforce. The financial loss related to Zap-Mail was substantial and probably could have been mitigated against if we had given 1,300 people two weeks notice. But the decision was management's, and every one of those people had worked tirelessly to make ZapMail work. ... There was no way we weren't going to make good on our no-layoff philosophy."[15]

> [Layoffs] never entered our minds. Our philosophy very simply is that it is a very short-term thing to do. If your focus is on the long term, the well-being of your business and its people, you don't do it.
>
> —Herb Kelleher

## RHINO FOODS

One of the best examples we've seen of dealing with a temporary overstaffing situation comes from tiny six-million-dollar Rhino Foods, a Vermont-based specialty frozen dessert, ice-cream novelty, and ice-cream ingredient manufacturer. In the spring of 1993, the job security of Rhino's 60 employees was seriously threatened by an unexpected drop in sales and a simultaneous increase in operating efficiency.

Rather than fold his hand or attempt to deal with the problem alone, Rhino President Richard Foos asked his employees to come up with a solution. Within three weeks, members of the company's Overcapacity Task Force came back with a novel yet downright business-like solution. Through the Employee Exchange Program, as they called it, Rhino workers would be farmed out to work at neighboring companies in the Burlington area which were experiencing temporary employment demand. Working only with companies which shared a common business philosophy and employment practices, Rhino provided its people with benefit and seniority continuity, in addition to making up any loss in wages. (Companies participating in the program included outfits like Gardener's Supply Co., and Ben & Jerry's Homemade, Inc. of nearby Waterbury.) Employees whose interim jobs paid more than their regular ones were allowed to keep the difference. Since successfully navigating through these troubled times, Rhino's sales and earnings have reportedly grown somewhere around 600 percent.

**RHINO FOODS**

|                    | 1990    | 1993      |
| ------------------ | ------- | --------- |
| EMPLOYEES          | 13      | 60        |
| SALES              | 890,000 | 6,000,000 |
| SALES PER EMPLOYEE | 68,462  | 100,000   |

*Source:* Foundation for Enterprise Development, 1997.

*I feel that in general terms it (the HP way) is the policies and actions that flow from the belief that men and women want to do a good job, a creative job, and that if they are provided the proper environment they will do so.*
—Bill Hewlett, HP co-founder

## CHAPTER SUMMARY

1. If you care about your people, you're there when times are tough.

   **Best Practices:**

   1. Ryder System, Inc. and Hurricane Andrew.

   2. Aaron Feuerstein rebuilding Malden Mills.

   3. Fred Gang's is "more than a paycheck."

2. Provide some system of justice. If you don't, someone else will do it for you.

   **Best Practice:**

   Suburban Propane's EARS Program.

3. Don't expect your employees to pay for your mistakes.

   **Best Practices:**

   1. Rhino Foods' Overcapacity Task Force.

   2. FedEx's handling of employees from its failed ZapMail project.

# TAKE CARE OF THE LITTLE THINGS

*I enjoin you to be ever alert to the pitfalls of too much authority. Beware that you do not fall in the category of the little man with a little job, with a big head. In essence, be considerate, treat your subordinates right, and they will literally die for you.*

—Major General Melvin Zais, U.S. Army

## WHERE EVERYBODY KNOWS YOUR NAME

Whether you like the man or not, Jimmy Johnson has demonstrated an uncanny knack for winning in the NFL. His two Superbowl victories less than five years after entering the league obviously were impressive enough credentials for Miami Dolphins team owner Wayne Huiezenga to hire Johnson to replace the legendary Don Shula—the winningest coach in the history of professional football.

Prior to his arrival in Miami, Johnson pointed to some really basic things that coaches, managers, and CEOs ought to be doing, but in many cases aren't. Like just getting to know your players' names, for instance. According to Johnson, "Some coaches bring their rookies into camp and, though they might know their first and second round picks by name, take the approach with the lower round picks and free agents that 'I'll learn his name if he makes the team.' What some don't understand is that whether a player makes the team might hinge on something as subtle as whether you know his name and whether you treat him as an individual that you care about, with talent you believe in."[1]

To us, (and perhaps to you as well) it seems totally absurd to be taking up time and space even mentioning this, except for one thing: It happens! As a case in point, one of our clients, an oth- erwise exceptionally well-run multi-billion dollar firm has for years experienced turnover in excess of 50 percent within its 3,000-plus member direct sales force. The turnover figure for newly hired reps (less than six months of service) exceeds 70 percent. Because of the high body count, company insiders have openly admitted that "we don't really bother getting to know them all that well because they're not going to be here very long." Better look inside your own organization for signs of sim- ilar attitudes.

> *Whether a player makes the team might hinge on some- thing as subtle as whether you know his name and whether you treat him as an individual that you care about, with talent you believe in.*

We call them "little things" because in the overall scheme of things, that's exactly what they are. They're no big deal—to you. But quite often, they are of huge importance to the employee(s) concerned, and can absolutely mean the difference when it comes to whether or not someone is really going to extend them- selves for you and your organization.

Among *Contented Cow* companies, examples of the personal touch abound. Here are a few of our favorites: Art Seessel, pres- ident of Seessel's Supermarkets (a Memphis-based regional gro- cery) regularly took time to send personal congratulatory notes to his employees for their "off-hours" accomplishments. One such note went to David Dettelbach, a part-time produce clerk, congratulating him on his high school athletic accomplish- ments. For years, Lucille Packard (widow of HP's David) per- sonally shopped for and bought small presents commemorating employee weddings and childbirths. Dennis LeStrange, of IKON

Office Solutions, personally sends birthday cards to each of his 1,300 employees. In each case the message is clear: They see their respective employees as more than merely a pair of hands sorting produce, assembling printers, or fixing copiers.

## THE NEED TO HAVE (SOME) FUN

Earlier we talked about the incredibly long hours logged by Netscape engineers ("When Too Much Work is Not Enough"). Since its inception, the entire software industry has been notorious for its workaholic standards. We suspect a problem may develop if such extended workdays have in fact become the "unwritten rule" (even if you can shoot billiards in the lounge). It will be interesting to see if dwelling in your office will become part of the job description, or whether future generations of software engineers will revolt.

In the meantime, late 1996 labor and employment figures for northern Florida showed a negative 3 percent unemployment rate for the area's computer programmers.[2] Statistically, that means every computer programmer in the region had a job, and 3 percent of them were *moonlighting*. Imagine that. Are we talking an employee's market, or what? So it's not surprising that David Graham, CEO of Jacksonville's InTuition, Inc.—the student loan servicer—was nervous about his company's ability to retain its topnotch technical employees during a 15-month, make-it-or-break-it conversion to all new software and hardware. When it was all over, however, the project was such a resounding success that it won the 1996 Project Management Institute's *Project of the Year Award*. Graham rewarded those responsible not only with a substantial bonus, but more to our point, with a gala dinner at an elegant yacht club. "We work hard," says Graham, echoing a theme voiced many times by Southwest's Herb Kelleher, "but we have to have fun."

We heard about the need to have some fun from lots of people in successful companies. Betty Kahn, of Chicago-based Crate & Barrel, a retailer of home furnishings says, "This is a partying company. We do a lot of group eating."[3] And it's not just at special events that the atmosphere of fun seems to make a difference. If you know anything about retail sales jobs, you know the associates at Crate & Barrel aren't working in retail to get rich quick; they're there because they're having fun.

Often the work and the fun are hard to distinguish between. Crate & Barrel managers are notorious for doing things like tying a lottery ticket or a couple of movie passes to the handle of a broom for the benefit of the first person to pick the thing up and use it. This kind of thinking is par for the course at Crate & Barrel, a standout in both employee and customer satisfaction in the specialty retail market.

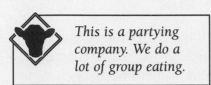

*This is a partying company. We do a lot of group eating.*

## RANDOM ACTS OF GRACE AND KINDNESS

Thong Lee, former laundry worker and now a bartender at the Seattle Marriott, will likely never forget the day that his boss, Sandy Olson, shut down the hotel's laundry for an entire day so the whole staff could attend his mother's funeral. Today, Lee proudly proclaims that he "puts on this uniform, just like an NBA player."[4]

In their absolutely delightful book, *NUTS*, about Southwest Airlines, authors Kevin and Jackie Freiberg offer an example on a somewhat grander scale. It seems that one day, Southwest Executive Vice President Colleen Barrett called into her office an employee who recently had been featured in some "not so glowing" customer letters. When asked if everything was okay, the employee apparently broke into tears and proceeded to describe a recent painful divorce, a custody battle over a 3-year-old child, and on top of that, an insurmountable $1,800 legal bill. A few hours later, the employee received an envelope with nothing but her name scrawled on it, and $1,800 in cash drawn from Colleen's personal account. Her reaction, aside from many subsequent years of loyal service? "At what other company could you walk in thinking you're fired and walk out feeling loved, listened to, and really cared about?"[5]

## CHAPTER SUMMARY

In the final analysis, it's frequently the "little things" which demonstrate whether or not you care. Little things like:

1. Just knowing people's names!

2. Making the effort to call attention to things which are important to people, like their birthdays, anniversaries, and accomplishments outside of work.

3. Knowing when to have some fun!

4. Regularly committing random acts of grace and kindness, on your own time, with your own money, and by sticking your own neck out for people.

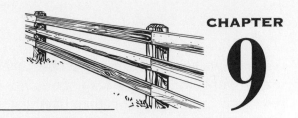

# A Case for Some Useful Benefits

*Everything has changed but for the way we think.*

—Albert Einstein

## ALL IN THE FAMILY

In the majority of American households today, both Mom and Dad go off to work for at least 40 hours a week. But wait! What happened to the woman who used to stay at home and do all the stuff that has to be done in the house? The cleaning, the laundry, taking care of sick kids, waiting for the exterminator or the oven repair guy, the grocery shopping, and, oh yeah, the cooking? Well, her position has been eliminated, but not the duties. So just as in corporate America, everybody has to pitch in and do the extra work in their spare time.

The term *Work/Life Balance* has been used to describe these changing patterns of human behavior, and that term works well for us. Lots of people out there want both. So many, in fact, that if you don't do some things to attract these people, your competitors will get them, the good ones at least. Ellen Galinksy, director of The Families and Work Institute, a non-profit research organization in New York, says that companies which respond to the need to adapt work to people's lives will win workers' loyalty, and with that, a competitive edge.[1]

We have all seen many programs that come under the heading of Work/Life. We think the programs are far less important, repeat, *far* less important, than having a clear understanding of what you wish to accomplish with respect to those workers who also happen to have a life. It means looking at the changing reality of your employees' lives away from the workplace. Why? You do it because you want to continue to be productive under a whole new set of rules and realities. In fact, we don't really even like the term "family friendly," but prefer the more accurate "family responsive." If you have to do things differently now to be successful in response to the role of today's family, then it makes sense to do them.

> *The programs are far less important, repeat, far less important, than having a clear understanding of what you wish to accomplish.*

Before you institute any of the programs or practices we'll describe, however, make sure you have some clearly defined Work/Life goals. We think a good Work/Life program, or system, should be designed to:

- Improve productivity.
- Attract the best people for the jobs you need done.
- Increase retention.
- Improve customer service, period.

Whenever considering any family-responsive measures, it only makes sense to do a business case analysis, comparing the costs with the benefits of the proposal. Don't use other people's data; do the analysis yourself, based on your own situation.

It may be hard to quantify the benefits of family responsiveness, but there are plenty of successful companies which have both quantifiable and anecdotal evidence that have convinced them they were doing the smart thing for the success of the enterprise:

- First Tennessee Bank, for example, found that supervisors rated by their employees as family-responsive retained employees twice as long as the bank average and kept 7 percent more retail customers. This, the bank says, contributed to a 55 percent profit gain over two years, to $106 million.[2]

• Fel-Pro, a Skokie, Illinois, gasket maker, reports that employees who take advantage of its family programs were more likely to participate in team problem-solving, and nearly twice as likely to suggest product or process improvements.[3]

• Aetna Life and Casualty cut in half its resignations by new mothers when it extended its unpaid parental leave to six months, and saved a million dollars a year in hiring and training expenses.[4] (The Families and Work Institute found that absenteeism for those using work/life benefits was 50 percent less than that for the workforce as a whole.)[5]

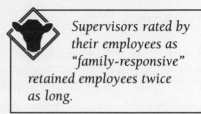

*Supervisors rated by their employees as "family-responsive" retained employees twice as long.*

• Boston-based John Hancock Financial Services says its family programs save the company approximately $500,000 each year in reduced turnover and absenteeism.[6]

## AVERAGE LENGTH OF EMPLOYMENT SERVICE IN YEARS

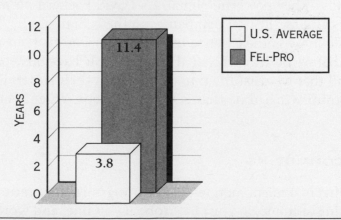

*Source:* Fel-Pro, U.S. Bureau of Labor Statistics.

While there are many interesting practices among the family-responsive policies adopted by American organizations, we'd like to look at four of them:

- Flextime
- Telecommuting
- Job-Sharing
- Child care accommodations

## FLEXTIME

In the least structured flextime programs, people work about 40 hours a week. It doesn't matter which 40, as long as they get the work done. Other flextime plans are more rigid; they simply are not bound by the traditional 8–5 time frame. For instance, you may work from 6:00AM to 3:00PM, or from 10:00AM to 7:00PM.

For some workers, especially those with school-age children and a spouse, flextime provides a major convenience, and for many companies, it requires practically nothing to accommodate. It's probably the least costly of the practices we looked at. As with all of these practices, having it on the "menu" and actually making it available to people can be two very different things.

Despite its apparent simplicity and nominal cost, this practice sends a very powerful signal. As David Packard pointed out (HP was among the first companies in the U.S. to use it), "To my mind, flextime is the essence of respect for and trust in people. It says that we both appreciate that our people have busy personal lives and that we trust them to devise, with their supervisor and work group, a schedule that is personally convenient yet fair to others."[7]

## TELECOMMUTING

Somewhat of a misnomer, telecommuting isn't commuting at all; it's staying at home, in your bathrobe if you like, and working by way of technology. Millions of workers telecommute regularly, according to Telecommute America, the non-profit group assembled to study and promote the practice. In 1996, 25 percent more Fortune 1000 corporations offered telecommuting arrangements than had made them available in 1995, but Telecommute America is quick to point out that telecommuting is not for everyone. It seems to work best when the job is one in which the employee is compensated on the basis of results, not activity, and when the worker is highly Committed already.

Salespeople and computer programmers make up the largest segment of the regular telecommuting population. (Translation: "We have rented out your office or cubicle to someone else."), but other professions are joining the fray every year. Temporary telecommuting arrangements have worked well in cases of a new mother easing back into work after childbirth, or during periods of partial convalescence following illness or surgery. Some people telecommute only occasionally, like when a child stays home sick, or during severe weather. In these cases, it can be very productive to be set up for telecommuting so that employees can take advantage of it should the need arise from time to time.

Telecommuting is not only a nice benefit to offer workers whose jobs and whose temperaments can handle it, it can also save big bucks in office overhead, and offer real gains in productivity. And that's what interests us. When the claims staff of the Hartford, Connecticut, office of Aetna Life and Casualty began telecommuting, the company recorded a 30 percent increase in the number of claims processed annually.[8]

Beware the perils of telecommuting, though, and they are worth considering. Such arrangements can clearly pose a threat to teamwork. The work of telecommuting groups has to be managed differently. Telecommuters and their managers have to make deliberate efforts to communicate clearly, since it probably won't happen on its own. Another danger involves overlooking outstanding talent or performance just because you don't see the person in the office very often. Though formidable, these considerations are far from insurmountable.

## AETNA – TOTAL REVENUE

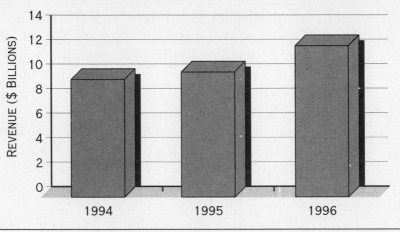

*Source:* Aetna Annual Report, 1996.

## JOB SHARING

Though not yet very popular, job sharing offers real benefits to both employers and employees who take advantage of it. In job sharing, (usually) two people simply split a regular full-time job. Each partner works slightly more than half the week to allow for some overlap and hand-off time. In the U.S., many job sharers are people who would simply opt out of the workforce if job sharing were not available. Companies that use job sharing often do so as an important and viable alternative to losing good talent.

You might say, "Nobody would really leave a job because of an inflexible work schedule." Think again. At the Chubb Group of Insurance Companies, a 1991 work/family needs analysis determined that of 7,800 U.S. employees, 60 percent were in dual-career families. About 50 percent had child or eldercare responsibilities, and another 20 percent anticipated having such responsibilities within three years. Almost one-third of employees who left the company in that year said in exit interviews that they did so to help them balance their work and family lives.[9]

Here's one example of how job sharing works. We have a friend who, along with a job sharing partner, is the head librarian in a large city library. She works 22 hours a week, all day Monday and Tuesday, and until 2:00PM on Wednesday. Her job sharing partner arrives each Wednesday morning at 11:00, and works out the remainder of the week. From 11:00AM to 2:00PM on Wednesday, partner #1 "hands off" any tasks and information partner #2 needs, and then the other hand off usually happens by phone over the weekend.

As good as job sharing might sound, it is the least used of the four practices we looked at. While 74 percent of employers represented on The Conference Board's Work-Family Roundtable offer job-sharing, less than 1 percent of their employees participate, a survey of the 155 companies shows.[10] The biggest problem seems to be the subtle, unwritten resistance of managers, and the intangible political downsides. We have to wonder if this isn't a little like the age-old mystery of the tree falling in an unpopulated forest. If you offer a benefit, and no one takes it, is it really offered?

Job sharing isn't for everyone. In fact, there are probably more jobs that wouldn't qualify than those that would. But consider this scenario: You have a really great employee whose job is well suited to job sharing and he or she wants to job share. The job sharing arrangement is disallowed, either explicitly or implicitly, by sending the message that this would be career suicide. Therefore, the person decides to leave. Who's better off?

## CHILD CARE BENEFITS

No other family-responsive practice is more complicated than that of child care. Some companies offer referral services, a practically free, and frankly, not very valuable service to employees. Others are on the opposite extreme, and operate on-site child care facilities. Most fall somewhere in the middle by offering child care subsidies at nearby facilities. Whatever your organization decides to do about child care, if anything, you should be mindful of the cost of doing nothing.

The Chubb companies became concerned about the fact that 50 exempt employees had left the company between 1992 and 1993 because of child care issues. Chubb knew that in its industry, it cost 97 percent of salary to replace the average employee. In the case of exempt employees, the average replacement cost was estimated at 150 percent of salary. On the basis of this data, it cost Chubb more than $3 million to replace the 50 exempt employees who left the company in 1992 and 1993 for child care reasons.[11]

And those who stay employed, but are constantly grappling with child care problems, are probably costing you even more than those who leave. According to Dun & Bradstreet, the annual cost to U.S. businesses of time lost through a breakdown in child care arrangements is about $3 billion![12] Nixon, Helms, and White in the *Journal of Compensation and Benefits*, report that about 5,000 U.S. parents reject work each *day* because they cannot find adequate or affordable child care.[13] If the job engine of a strong economy continues to roar, driving the unemployment rate further south, this will become even more of an issue.

One way companies have addressed the problem is by building and operating on-site child care facilities. For the eighth consecutive year, SAS Institute Inc., the Cary, North Carolina, software developer we mentioned earlier, has been recognized by *Working Mother* magazine as one of the "100 Best Companies for Working Mothers." Inclusion on the 11th annual list was based in part upon its family-responsive practices, including on-site child care. "Women comprise almost half of our workforce so we are very sensitive to issues specific to women in the workplace," said David Russo, vice president of human resources for SAS Institute. "SAS continues to set the pace for catering to the needs of employees engaged in both pursuing a career and raising a family."[14]

With employee turnover at 4 percent, versus an industry average of almost 20 percent, SAS Institute must be doing something right. Since its founding in 1976, the company has become the world's ninth largest independent software company, growing 526 percent in the last 10 years alone, and consistently wins honors for being a company full of *Contented Cows*.

But is on-site child care always the answer? Not necessarily. Construction of a new child care center is expensive, usually half a million to a million dollars, and you'll need a steady supply of at least 75 children to make it break even, says Marguerite W. Sallee, CEO of Nashville's Corporate Child Care Management Service Inc.[15] Besides, if you're not in the child care business, you really should outsource the management of the center. Moreover, child care experts warn that on-site child care is often the only alternative considered, and then often rejected because of the cost and impracticality of the proposal.[16] In many cases, further probing has discovered that flexible hours or part-time arrangements were of more value to employees than a big fancy child care facility.

## GO ASK YOUR PEOPLE

Flextime, telecommuting, job sharing, on-site child care. These are four programs that can make a difference. IF they are seen as valuable by your employees. IF they reduce stress, turnover, hiring, and training costs. IF they allow your employees to serve your customers better. But don't limit your thinking to those areas.

You will have more success with family responsiveness if you ask and expect employees to take responsibility for their own family issues, and then partner with them to provide ways to address the needs of the family. Companies which opt instead to take responsibility for all their employees' family choices will both fail at it and live to regret *their choice*.

Ask your employees, "What are you struggling with all the time? What would make your life easier? So much easier that it would enable you to make a substantially greater contribution to what we do here?"

Chubb asked questions like these and, as a result, came up with a solution to "Snow Days" at its Warren, New Jersey, headquarters. Several days each winter, schools would be closed for weather reasons, but businesses, including Chubb, were going strong. On these days, Chubb allows parents to bring children ages 5 to 12 to work. Caregivers supervise the children from 8:00AM to 5:00PM in training and conference rooms. Activities include arts

## CHUBB INSURANCE GROUP

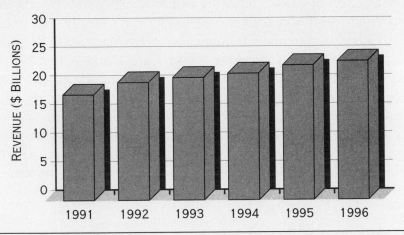

*Source:* Chubb Insurance Group.

and crafts, reading, physical play in the company's fitness center, and board games. With virtually no cost to the company, parents pay a one-time registration fee of $25, plus $15 per day per child. The daily fee includes morning and afternoon snacks.[17]

## STARBUCKS: BUSINESS-MINDED BENEFITS

Since opening its first store in Seattle in 1971, Starbucks Coffee has grown to more than 1,200 stores and kiosks as of this writing (see Figure 9.1). Named one of *Fortune's* 100 Fastest Growing Companies in 1994, the company has experienced truly meteoric growth in both sales (650 percent) and earnings (900 percent) since going public (SBUX) in 1992. Chances are you've seen their mostly young, part-time workforce in action, serving up everything from a cup of plain black coffee to a "for-here, double-tall decaf, non-fat, no-whip amaretto mocha." It may be that the Starbucks "baristas," as they call their counter workers, pull their shots of espresso with such energy and animation because of some atmospherically generated caffeine high present in their storefront cafes. Or, it may be because they are simply pumped

**FIGURE 9.1**

STARBUCKS COFFEE COMPANY STORE LOCATIONS

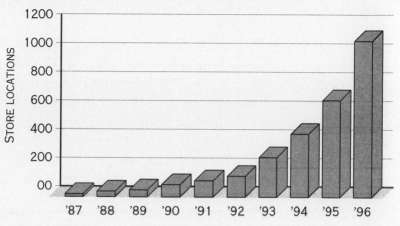

*Source:* Starbucks, 1997.

about working there. Part of the reason may have something to do with their exceptional benefits package.

As we pointed out earlier, there's no commercial wisdom in the notion that "more is better" when it comes to employee benefits. But at Starbucks, according to Senior Vice President of Human Resources Sharon Elliott, the benefits plan (which includes, among other features: health, dental and vision care, stock options, a 401(k), vacation, and a weekly pound of coffee), "more than pays for itself."[18]

In the fast-service restaurant business, employee longevity averages somewhere in the vicinity of four months. By comparison, the average Starbucks barista is on the job one and a half years, with more than a few staying for up to nine years. And those who stick with it can amass a respectable fortune, not from the $6–$7 an hour in base pay, but from "Bean Stock," the company's innovative employee ownership plan. An employee who stays at Starbucks for five years or more can accumulate enough stock to make a down payment on a house. Says Corey Rosen, director of the National Center for Employee Ownership, "That can make a difference for the rest of their lives."[19]

At least three features are worth noting about the benefits plan at Starbucks:

- Given the company's heavy dependence on a largely part-time workforce and the desire to retain skilled baristas, Starbucks apparently sees some wisdom in treating their part-timers like "real people" when it comes to benefits eligibility. (After a 90-day waiting period, both full and part-time employees are eligible.)
- Perhaps the most novel aspect of their approach to benefits is that the plans were designed not by some guy with a green eye shade in lower Manhattan, but by the employees themselves. As Howard Schultz, president and ceo (all Starbucks titles are lower cased) explains, "Since our partners are the ones who use, and are most affected by the health-care plan, asking them to help develop a tailored plan was the only way to achieve our goal."[20]
- Finally, and surprisingly, given the plan's origin, employees pay one-third of the cost, with the company contributing the remaining two-thirds. Consistent with the theme of this book, good benefit plans are a shared obligation, not a gift. (That which costs me nothing has little value.)

## (ALMOST) EVERYTHING UNDER ONE ROOF

Your workplace may have a cafeteria, even a bank, or some other little conveniences to keep you from having to go offsite for life's daily routines. Here are a few simple adjustments that have made a big difference for the *Contented Cows* who dreamed them up.

- Do you have a car repair facility onsite where you work? You do if you work at the "Taj Mahal," as EDS's Plano, Texas, World Headquarters is affectionately known. The compound's garage, along with its bank, store, day care center, and dry cleaners save employees tons of time over the course of a year, and it makes them more present, literally, on the job, and more productive.
- Pharmaceuticals maker Rhône-Poulenc Rorer offers a multitude of on-site services—including a shoe repair service, dry cleaners, car servicing, jewelry repair service, floral service, shuttle buses and vans, and a 400-square-foot company store—designed to allow employees to tend to errands without leaving

## RHÔNE-POULENC NET INCOME

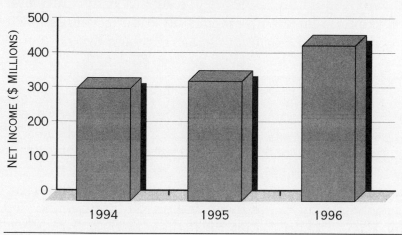

*Source:* Rhone-Poulenc, 1996 annual report.

work. The company has found that employees stay at work longer if they don't need to rush out to do errands.[21] Makes sense to us.

• PepsiCo offers "concierge" services to help employees with errands and tasks that need to be done during the workday—such as getting an oil change, lining up an evening babysitter, or contracting for house repairs. The employer has found that by taking care of these tasks (which were once handled by the "housewives" of a bygone era), it can help employees keep their minds on their work. As a result, PepsiCo has a more focused workforce.[22]

• Take-home meals provide another example of doing something smart to make life just a little easier for people. Retailer Eddie Bauer, enjoying annual sales growth of 20 percent, and drug maker Rhône-Poulenc Rorer, both keep the company cafe open late to prepare individual or family meals for harried employees to take home.[23] (P.S. It's also not a bad way to supplement the bottom line of what is typically a money-losing operation.)

• At Fel-Pro, the first shift runs from 7:24AM to 3:54PM. Why such an odd schedule? A company-commissioned study of the traffic patterns in the area of the plant found that this schedule would enable first-shifters to shorten their commute times and help them avoid traffic hassles. The result? A marked decrease in lateness and an increase in productivity and effectiveness.[24] We never said it took an Einstein to figure out these things.

## CHAPTER SUMMARY

If you care about your people, you provide benefits which are truly beneficial—to you, to them, and to your bottom line. You recognize, for example, that the family is changing. If you respond in ways that help people care for their families, they can be more productive.

1. Four ways to be family-responsive are to provide:
   - Flextime
   - Telecommuting
   - Job-sharing
   - Child-care options

2. Before launching into any kind of benefit, find out what people want. Go ask 'em; don't assume! Do a business case analysis. Do your own homework. Make changes for business reasons, not good corporate PR.

**Best Practices:**

1. SAS Institute's on-site child care.
2. Starbucks Coffee's benefits and stock ownership plan for both full- and part-time employees.
3. Fel-Pro's commuter-friendly shifts.
4. On-site personal services at EDS and Rhône-Poulenc Rorer.

# SECTION FOUR

## CONTENTED COWS ARE ENABLED

$$\left(\begin{array}{c}\text{Enabled – To provide with the}\\ \text{Means or Opportunity}\end{array}\right)$$

# EMPOWER THIS!

*When the systems, structure, policies, procedures and practices of an organization are designed and lived out so that employees genuinely feel they come first, trust is the result.*

—Jackie and Kevin Freiberg, *NUTS*

## THE RECENT ETYMOLOGY OF A BUZZWORD

In August of 1979, I first used a word in a speech in New York that I had never heard used within the context of employee relations. However, over the last 18 years, the use of that same word in the business lexicon has reached virus-like proportions. In the process, the term has taken on a life (and many new definitions) of its own. Sadly, as is too often the case with any product, image, or even a humble word which somehow makes the journey from obscurity to ubiquity, we see entire books, seminars, tapes, lectures, T-shirts, and ballcaps devoted to it. There's nothing wrong with that, except for the fact that with every mindless repetition, its meaning gets hopelessly muddled, if not lost altogether. The word?

*Empowered.*

The reason for discussing empowerment is even more crucial now than it was in 1979. Even as managers rush around doing whatever they do to "empower" their people, many are headed entirely in the wrong direction. Your people may not really need "empowering" at all. Think about it. They know how to find their way to work. For the most part, they not only know what their jobs are, but also the best ways of doing them. Management professor Henry Mintzberg offers an analogy. "Consider," he says, "a truly advanced social system: the beehive. Queen bees don't empower worker bees. The worker bees are adults, so to speak, who know exactly what they have to do. Indeed, the queen bee has no role in the genuinely strategic decisions of the hive, such as the one to move on to a new location. The bees decide collectively, responding to the informative dances of the scouts. ... What the queen bee does is exude a chemical substance that holds the system together. She is responsible for what has been called the *spirit* of the hive."[1]

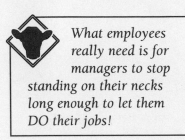

*What employees really need is for managers to stop standing on their necks long enough to let them DO their jobs!*

Our experience has shown that what most employees really need is for managers to stop standing on their necks long enough to let them DO their jobs! In short, what they need is for us to stop *dis*empowering them.

A pivotal concept of those remarks back in 1979 was that successful organizations went to truly great lengths to ensure that they were hiring only those who were "qualified" for the position in question, and equipped by virtue of temperament, ideology, and attitude to be successful and content within the organization.

With that vital first step established, it was then equally important to ensure that these spanking new, highly qualified, and motivated troops were equipped with the "whys and wherefores" of the organization, and firmly pointed to a target. "Crack troops" don't tolerate standing at parade rest or aimlessly wandering very well. In fact, they become dangerous, both to themselves and those around them.

In order to be truly effective, we've got to make sure our people are totally and completely equipped to do their jobs and then (and only then) get ourselves (and the organization) out of their way! Stand aside and let them work!

We're not about to suggest that getting people to assume additional responsibility is easy. It's not. Some folks (and this isn't confined to the lower echelons) *like* being told what to do. But the real problem as we see it is that too many managers enjoy satisfying that wish. And because they enjoy it, they're good at it. They start by hiring people who *need* to be told what to do, and then tell them in every way imaginable that they don't want them to think or take responsibility. Requiring people to take responsibility for their work and allowing them to define and solve problems requires them to amend, among other things, both their roles, and, once again, their expectations.

*We've got to take out the boss element.*

—Jack Welch

## IDENTIFYING FOUR TYPES OF MANAGERS

In their letter to shareholders published in the company's 1995 annual report, GE Executive Officers Jack Welch, Paolo Fresco, and John Opie crystallized the problem we're attempting to pinpoint:

> It was at Work-Out sessions that it became clear that some of the rhetoric heard at the corporate level—about involvement and excitement and turning people loose—did not match the reality of life in the businesses. The problem was that some of our leaders were unwilling, or unable, to abandon big-company, big-shot autocracy and embrace the values we were trying to grow. So we defined our management styles, or "types,"* and how they furthered or blocked our values. And then we acted.
>
> Type I [the Contented Cow] not only delivers on performance commitments, but believes in and furthers GE's small-company values. The trajectory of this group is "onward and upward," and

---

* Coincidentally, GE's "types" correspond to descriptions historically used in bovine classification. (See J. Albright, op. cit.) Hence, these "cow-nterparts" are included in brackets [].

*the men and women who comprise it will represent the core of our
senior leadership into the next century.*

*Type II [the Slow Milker, Chronic Kicker, or Finicky Eater] does
not meet commitments, nor share our values—nor last long at GE.*

*Type III [the Fence-Breaking Explorer] believes in the values but
sometimes misses commitments. We encourage taking swings, and
Type III is typically given another chance.*

*Type IV [the Boss Cow]. The "calls" on the first two types are easy.
Type III takes some judgment; but Type IV is the most difficult. One
is always tempted to avoid taking action, because Type IV's deliver
short-term results. But Type IV's do so without regard to values and,
in fact, often diminish them by grinding people down, squeezing
them, stifling them. Some of these learned to change; most couldn't.
The decision to begin removing Type IV's was a watershed—the
ultimate test of our ability to "walk the talk," but it had to be done
if we wanted GE people to be open, to speak up, to share, and to act
boldly outside traditional "lines of authority" and "functional boxes"
in this new learning, sharing environment."[2]*

## ONE BAD APPLE CAN SPOIL THE WHOLE BARREL

Hundreds of contenders abound in the wings, waiting to accept
the accolades and financial rewards associated with *Contented
Cow* stature. But many of these companies fail to progress
beyond the "wannabe" stage, precisely because of a few, or
maybe just one, of the aforementioned Type IV managers. The
efforts of the legitimate *Contented Cow* managers are severely
diluted, if not obliterated, by these few "bad apples."

Look around. Maybe you're feeling pretty smug about the
contentedness of your workforce in general, but do you notice a
pocket of your organization with uncharacteristically high tur-
moil and turnover? It's possible they're still making their numbers. But it *might* be worth taking a closer look.

In more than one company we've examined, we've seen the
valiant efforts of lots of well-intentioned leaders completely over-
shadowed by one or two Boss Cows. But, because they were
achieving short-term results, albeit at the expense of people in

their areas, it was tough for anyone to summon the courage to do anything about it.

It's not just the damage these Type IV's do within their own departments. Greater destruction by far occurs elsewhere in the organization, when people see this type of behavior tolerated or even encouraged. There seems to be a mixed message that sounds like this: "Our people are our most important assets. Really, they are. And our practice is to treat people in ways that will motivate them to stellar performance. We realize we've got one or two managers around here who don't get it. That's okay, because they're turning in the needed results right now. If you're not under their control, don't worry about them. Just be glad you don't work for them. If you do happen to work for them ... well ... it's a free world."

That just won't work. The glaring inconsistency involving even just a few will undermine and mitigate the valiant efforts of the majority. Once again, it is an all-or-nothing proposition. You're either Committed or you aren't. Remember, this is not a quest for the "moral high ground." It's just plain good business, and if there is any doubt, go back to Chapter 1 and revisit GE's financials.

If upon looking around, you discover a couple of these folks in your organization, you owe it to them (and everyone else) to be very clear about about your commitment to these principles. If they choose not to sign on, cull them from the herd, now. Do it professionally and humanely, but do it!

## GIVE PEOPLE BACK THEIR WORK

As currently viewed, empowerment is something which is bestowed on those whose boxes on the organization chart are south of our own. Consistent with this plantation mindset, if it were not granted to them, they wouldn't have it. Now, contrast that with some situations where workers truly *do* have a high degree of influence (control, if you will) over their work and the work environment. Three that come readily to mind are those involving physicians, commercial airline pilots, and professional

basketball players. In all three cases, the workers are well empowered already, with no thanks to either a manager or any sort of
empowerment program.

Do you really think, for example, that a Delta Air Lines pilot
needs special empowerment from the chief pilot (or anybody else
at Delta) to request a different altitude to avoid some thunder
cells, or that your doctor needs additional empowering from a
hospital administrator to order a chest X-ray? Or, can you imagine Chicago Bulls coach Phil Jackson calling a special practice or
a timeout during a game for the purpose of empowering Michael
Jordan, Scottie Pippen, or (heaven forbid) Dennis Rodman to
pass the ball, take a shot, or run a different play than the one
which had been called? Of course not, and the reason is that
whatever empowering is going on took place long ago, when it
was baked into the person's job.

> *No profit grows where is no pleasure ta'en. ...*
>
> —Shakespeare

## CHAPTER SUMMARY

1. Stop trying to "empower" your people. You'll only drive
   them (and yourself) crazy trying to figure it out. It's far
   easier and more beneficial to find those things which
   serve to *dis*empower them (dumb policies and procedures, managerial behaviors, etc.) and eradicate them.
   Do it with a vengeance!

2. Hire people who truly want to take responsibility for
   their work, then get out of their way!

3. Painful as it may be in the short run, either convert the
   "Boss Cows" to a new style of management or help them
   find a new job ... preferably with a competitor.

# ENABLED EMPLOYEES ARE INCREDIBLY WELL TRAINED

*To try to build an organization against weakness frustrates the purpose of organization.*

—Peter Drucker

## WHY YOU CAN'T GET A PILOT'S LICENSE BY MAIL

Take a look inside the cockpit (er flight deck) of a modern jetliner. At first glance, one can't help but be astonished by all the instruments—the gauges, computers, screens, levers, dials, and the like. How the men and women who call that place their office keep it all straight is, in and of itself, a miracle.

However, for our purposes, what you in fact see up there is considerably less important than what you *don't* see, namely a supervisor or manager. Instead, there are two, maybe three people who, due to the vagaries of crew scheduling, probably don't know each other very well, but they do know exactly what their job is, and they know how to do it.

For those who need a numbers fix about now, consider this. Pound for pound, in terms of the ratio of "worker bees" per manager, commercial airline pilots are among the most productive employees you'll find anywhere. Typically, for the major commercial carriers, the number of crew members per manager is in excess of 100:1. Compare that to the span of control ratio in your (or most any other) business!

So how did they reach such levels of efficiency? Well, it's true perhaps that the airlines do enjoy an advantage insofar as being able to state the mission and goals for their flight crews in a simple, succinct fashion. The mission, for example is pretty clear:

> *Fly this plane and its passengers from New York's Kennedy Airport to Atlanta's Hartsfield Airport.*

So, too, the goals:

> *Do it safely, and as efficiently as possible.*

Sounds simple, right? But consider that there are probably a million things that could happen to that aircraft between New York and Atlanta. Therefore every single crew member who straps-in up front must be trained to deal with any eventuality.

Mind you, it's not that the airlines necessarily *want* to spend exorbitant amounts of time and money to ensure that their aircrews are trained to this degree of proficiency. Rather, they know they have to, because without it nobody in their right mind would get on the plane. Moreover, they are compelled by law to meet certain safety requirements. The problem with our more earthbound organizations is that we don't have anybody or anything scaring us enough to make us do it.

Many companies fund training efforts when times are good, then either slash or eliminate them entirely when times get tough. *Think for just a moment about the sheer stupidity of this concept: We have an earnings problem, so we're going to work our way out of it by "dumbing down" the organization with less skilled, less competent people! Now the only problem will be to find dumb customers to purchase our goods and services and even dumber investors to buy our stock!*

## TRAINING EXPANDS THE MEANING OF PROFESSIONALISM

So where is it written and why is it that just because they don't wear labcoats, epaulets, or attend Harvard, a waitress, machinist, sales clerk, assembly worker, or anyone else cannot or should not be viewed and treated as a professional, with all the attendant rights, privileges and, yes, responsibilities? In a sense, what we're advocating is that if you really want to maximize your employees' level of contribution, you treat them the same way the hospital does its doctors, the airline its pilots, the law firm its lawyers, and so forth—as *professionals*.

The pursuit of professionalism throughout an organization means, among other things, a commitment to training. One organization that doesn't cheat in this regard is Hewlett-Packard which, according to co-founder David Packard, spends upwards of a half-billion dollars annually—a sum which equates to nearly 2 percent of revenue— training its 98,000 employees.[1]

> *If you really want to maximize your employees' level of contribution, you treat them the same way the hospital does its doctors, the airline its pilots, the law firm its lawyers, and so forth—as professionals.*

USAA, the San Antonio based auto insurer, is a believer as well. Under former (1969-1993) President Robert McDermott, a retired Air Force brigadier general and former dean of the Air Force Academy, the company invested massively in employee training (as much as 3 percent of revenues). Judging by a 146-percent increase in the asset/employee ratio between 1985 and 1994, we'd say their ROI from this type of investment isn't too shabby at all.[2] And, since 1970, they've successfully lowered their employee turnover rate from 40 percent to 6 percent![3]

*An investment in knowledge always pays the best interest.*
—Ben Franklin

How much training could it possibly take to prepare a Starbucks barista to take the counter at one of the coffee chain's cafes? Would you believe 24 hours of formal classroom training, and 25 to 30 hours of practical onsite training?[4] To pour coffee?! No, but to learn to "call" the order using precisely the right syntax, to brew the coffee, pull shots of espresso, steam milk with varying fat content, and to learn "cup management," a mnemonic mechanism which uses the position of the cup and its handle to signal to the person preparing the drink exactly what was ordered. Never knew it was that complicated? Well, it is. And if you pride yourself, as Starbucks does, in providing an exceptional experience for the customer, you can increase your chances for success by providing exceptional training for those on the front line.

In 1995, the American Society for Training and Development conducted a survey to determine the amount of money (as a percent of payroll) that companies were spending on training. As indicated by the following graph, a majority of respondents (58 percent) were spending somewhere between 0 and 1.5 percent of payroll on their training efforts, and about a quarter of them were somewhere above 1.5 percent.[5] While one could make the argument that many appear at first glance to be seriously underfunded, at least by comparison to companies like HP and USAA (which are reportedly in the 2–3 percent of *revenue* range), the thing that shocked us the most about the study results was the fact that 16 percent of the respondents didn't even know what they were spending![6] (see Figure 11.1) *Do you?*

## THE HIDDEN COSTS OF IGNORED TRAINING

Let's look for a moment beyond the direct and obvious benefits. What is the cost of *not* providing needed training? More to the point, what is the cost of incompetence in any part of your organization? To be sure, there are direct costs. You pay an added price for re-work, lost customers, and yes, the cost of additional supervisors to run around looking over the shoulders of your motivated but marginally competent troops. But we believe there is a cost far greater and more debilitating than any of these, and

**FIGURE 11.1**

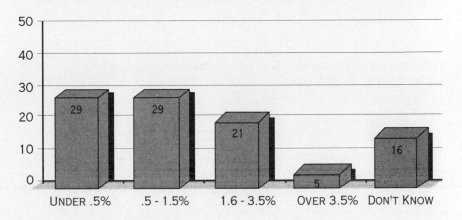

% OF COMPANY PAYROLL SPENT ON TRAINING & DEVELOPMENT

it has to do with what happens to the psyche and performance of your employees when they don't feel particularly competent, or confident in their ability to do something.

How many times in your life, usually in a customer interaction (where you're the customer), have you had a sales clerk, reservationist, waiter, or any employee for that matter, start the transaction with the words "I'm new at this. ..."? (*By the way, how would you like to hear those same words from your neurosurgeon as you're being wheeled into the operating room?*) In making that pronouncement, what that person really is saying to you and, more importantly to themselves is, "I'm probably gonna screw this up, so please be patient and understanding with me." And if a person *thinks* they will screw something up, guess what? They will! Moreover, if they screw it up this time, how confident are they going to be the next time? Your potentially contented, productive employee just became a very demoralized one, and for good reason. As Jimmy Johnson points out, "The coach or manager's job is to make the player feel as good about himself as he can possibly feel, all the time. You'd think every coach, manager, and CEO in America would understand this by now."[7]

Make no mistake about it. People who are proficient in their jobs and who *know* they will be competent enough to handle the difficult tasks ahead feel confident about themselves and stay calm and poised in on-the-spot crises. As a result, they perform better than an employee who never got a lesson in the basics.

## WALKING, TALKING CATALOGS AT CRATE & BARREL

Have you ever been to a Crate & Barrel, the home furnishings store? If so, you may have been surprised at how much each of their sales associates knows about every item in the store's vast inventory. That's because they do an incredibly good job of equipping each of their people with detailed knowledge about everything they sell. One of Crate & Barrel's top priorities is keeping salespeople fully informed of every available product. A new item hits the shelf only after associates have "read all about it," and for the really big lines and complicated items, each store receives a *Video Information Bulletin* which is required viewing for everyone in the store. Says C&B's Betty Kahn, "They have to know the product, so they can sell it."[8]

## AN INTELLIGENT LEARNING PROCESS

It's no surprise or coincidence that FedEx, GE, and Southwest have some of the most admired (and emulated) corporate universities in the world. Of far greater importance than the bricks and mortar behind these institutions is the level of personal commitment displayed by their respective CEOs. Each, for example, regularly makes time to visit the classroom, and, beyond merely waving the flag, participates meaningfully in the learning process. Anyone who has ever witnessed new managers jousting with Fred Smith in the "U," or Jack Welch in "the pit" at Crotonville knows there is some serious learning going on.

Without a doubt, the *Contented Cow* companies are deadly serious about the issue of training, an attitude that goes well beyond the amount of money they spend doing it, the impressiveness of their truly first rate learning facilities, the breadth of course offerings, and the like. Instead, we think what makes them special is that despite the success they've enjoyed or how big they may have become, they have not lost sight of one of the most fundamental precepts in the whole employee relations arena: The person who started work for them this morning is as close to a model employee as they're ever going to get. And unlike so many others who no doubt recognize the same thing, they actively (fanatically might be a better word for it) DO something about it.

While we have talked about orientations as an opportunity for employers to establish open, two-way communication with new hires from the outset, we cannot overemphasize the fact that orientations are primarily for training. Like many companies, Disney requires every single employee—no matter what their station in life—to attend a comprehensive new employee orientation (Disney Traditions). But the similarity ends there, because the focus is not so much on telling people where to find the paper clips, having them fill out forms until their fingers ache, or introducing them to dozens of new people who will likely be forgotten by lunchtime. Instead, they make sure the new cast member is carefully introduced to the company's traditions, philosophies, and a very different way of life—the Disney way.

Rosenbluth Travel, the giant travel agency, flies every newly hired Travel Sales Associate to its Philadelphia headquarters for an orientation. There the focus is on the company's beliefs, history, values, and goals. Following the orientation, the TSA's are then immersed in a comprehensive six to eight week training program before they are turned loose on paying customers.[9] How long do your managers and new hires spend with this process: an hour, maybe two?

Faced with problems that are becoming all too familiar, Marriott found it necessary to redefine the parameters of the traditional orientation, especially when faced with the question, "Where does training begin?" Heavily dependent upon low-wage workers (many of whom are recent immigrants from places like Bosnia and China, or fresh from the welfare rolls), the company has baked a lot of reality into its training regimen.

Marriott recognized that there were some rather elementary things—like speaking English, basic literacy, parenting (*that's caring for kids, not creating them*), work etiquette, and problem solving—many of their people needed to learn before teaching them how to do their job even became relevant. While some may argue that they've crossed the line into a whole new social order, Charles R. Romeo, director of employee benefits for ConAgra, puts it another way: "The burden is on us, not on the employee, to change. For many of us, that's a new recognition."[10]

## TRAINING TO PROFICIENCY: A WRONGHEADED APPROACH

Let's make an important distinction here. Spending a ton of money on training is *not* the issue. In fact, relative to the ROI for their training dollars, many organizations spend entirely too much time and money on training, either because they mistakenly view it as the answer for every performance or behavioral problem, or they've somehow been sucked into accepting the notion that training to proficiency (i.e., no wash-outs) is the way to go. Sadly, in many cases, it represents nothing more than throwing money at the issue, a practice which is unfailingly stupid.

## THE FAA: BLIND IN ONE EYE?

The Federal Aviation Agency (FAA) presents something of a case in point. In the past, newly hired air traffic controllers would all report to the organization's training academy in Oklahoma for their initial training and certification. Those who—with a reasonable amount of instruction over a reasonable period of time—couldn't pass muster went home to seek their fame and fortune elsewhere. At some point this practice was amended in favor of a train-to-proficiency approach, and the end result is that now nobody ever gets sent home or, as our friend Alex Nicholas calls it, de-selected. Instead, you wind up with a situation where people who would have washed out under the old system are *still* in training and on the job years later, and every day must have their work carefully overseen by an experienced controller. A competent employee ends up babysitting an inept one, making them both, at best, marginally productive; and both are making the same money!

Generally, this type of situation seems to arise either from some misguided thinking about the nature of the employment relationship, or because the training organization doesn't want to stand up and be held accountable for its efforts. We are firm advocates of taking pains to ensure that people are proficient in required job skills for the life of their job tenure. We're equally fervent in the belief that there is a point at which you realize "this dog won't hunt."

As very frequent flyers, we take considerable comfort in knowing that commercial aircrews are not only well trained, but that they must regularly (every six to 12 months) demonstrate their capability via a proficiency test. Pilots (and flight attendants) who don't pass those checks are grounded until they can. Sadly, we don't have the same confidence in the air traffic control system on which those pilots depend.

> There is a point at which you realize "this dog won't hunt."

## TRAINING UP A (DESERT) STORM

Prior to the start of hostilities in the 1991 Gulf War, General H. Norman Schwarzkopf kept his troops out in the desert for what seemed to many like an eternity. And it wasn't simply because he was waiting for the last diplomatic efforts to fail. They were there to train.

Of course, the U.S. Armed Forces had not gone out in the street and simply drafted the first half-million people who happened to be standing around. In the main, General Schwarzkopf's command consisted of well-equipped, professional soldiers who had already undergone months, if not years, of training. Many had experienced combat before. But it was important to the general not just to ensure that his soldiers were ready, but to get them to the point where *they* knew they were ready.

According to Schwarzkopf, the fact that his troops were a lot better equipped than their adversaries was nearly inconsequential. In an interview with David Frost shortly after the war, the general theorized that if the armament situation had been reversed, his troops would *still* have won as clearly and convincingly as they did, due largely to the psychological advantage. Nor can one underestimate the importance of the troops' knowing that Schwarzkopf had not whiled away the months in a cushy rear area waiting for the ground phase to begin; he had endured the desert with them.

## VISIBILITY MATTERS

All too often, a company decides to send people to a training program without first securing the buy-in of the organization's leadership. Like it or not, people want to know that the training course they're taking time to sit through is as important to senior management as it is supposed to be to them. Often that means senior management needs to sit through the same program as everyone else, not in their own condensed mini-versions, but right alongside all the others.

There should be no executive parking spaces when it comes to training. They must participate enthusiastically and, perhaps most importantly, they need to demonstrate the skills they expect everyone else to learn. Commenting on his participation in a 60-hour training class alongside other Rubbermaid employees, CEO Wolfgang Schmitt said, "I had to visibly be a part of it. People look to see if you just talk about it or actually do it."[11]

Not long ago, we conducted a workshop in Coaching Skills for a group of plant managers and superintendents for Florida Power Corporation. The session was conducted in a company training facility in the small town of Crystal River, about 100 miles north of the company's St. Petersburg headquarters. The vice president who brought us in, George Marks, underwent the training along with all of his direct reports. George's personal presence and participation in the training wasn't lost on anybody.

His willingness to be observed in a new situation—a vulnerable, "untrained state"—was appreciated by the other class members.

A few months later, George decided to bring us back to provide the same program for the next level of employees below his direct reports. Although he had already completed the training, he thought it was important to put his stamp of support on the program for this group. However, the scheduling that worked best for the attendees wasn't convenient for him. This particular day, he had an important budget meeting back in St. Petersburg, but because he thought it was important enough for him to kick off the training session, he took a company helicopter from St. Petersburg to Crystal River early that morning.

At 7:45AM, he landed at a small airport a half mile from the training site, then drove over to kick off the training program by telling the assembled group of the benefits he had realized since taking the course. After his talk, he and a Crystal River colleague got in a car and drove south to St. Petersburg. He made a 200-mile round trip to deliver a 10-minute message. What the employees gleaned from seeing their vice president standing in front of them and knowing the effort it took for him to be there was far more important than any single thing any of us said that day. The message had been sent, loud and clear: "This is important. It's so important that I went through it before you did. I'm using it, and now I want and expect you to do the same."

By contrast, we conducted several training sessions for a large Midwest manufacturer. Due to the conspicuous absence of any member of senior management throughout the entirety of this effort, we often heard the question, "If this is so important, where are they?" Months later, an informal survey of those who attended indicated that only a few people were using the skills we covered in the course. It's possible the senior officers didn't really need to be there for their personal benefit but, as we've heard so many times before, perception is reality. To us, it's a little like the difference between the parents who *send* versus *accompany* their children to church.

## A QUICK SELF-EXAM

Sadly, companies seldom go to the trouble of ensuring that the training efforts they've paid for have actually taught their people anything. Here are some questions we believe you should ask:

1. Have you established and do you train to minimum proficiency standards?
2. How must trainees *demonstrate* proficiency, both on an initial and recurrent basis? We're not just talking about skills training, either. Don't let anyone try to tell you that learned skills and acquired knowledge can't be reliably demonstrated. (While we're on the subject, why is it that no one ever flunks a corporate training program? Are both trainers and students *really* that good?)
3. What follow-up measures do you have in place to ensure that people have actually *learned* something from a training effort, and that they intend to use it?

One of our clients has implemented a simple but effective tool to work on this one. After a training class (which he and his entire senior management team usually attend first), his people receive a letter which asks them to describe for him in writing not only what they've learned, but how they intend to put it to use. (see below)

*Dear* _____:

*You have just completed a two day XYZ Skills Workshop sponsored by our company. My hope is that the workshop was a success, and that you are coming away armed with new skills which you can put to use.*

*My purpose in writing is to reinforce the expectation that the acquired skills/methods do, in fact, need to be put to use. Put simply, you and your fellow participants were provided this developmental opportunity because of the belief that it would lead to more productive and satisfied managers and work units.*

*Within the next week, I would like for you to provide me a brief (2 pages or less) written summary as to:*

- *What you learned;*
- *How you intend to apply it in the course of your every day job;*
- *What I (or other members of our management team) can do to support you in this regard;*
- *How, when, and by what means you plan to measure the relative success of these efforts.*

*Sincerely,*

*John Q. President*

4. Who pays for the training?

Some would argue that it makes no difference, as in the final analysis it all comes out of the same wallet anyhow. We disagree vehemently. If a training offering arrives as a gift of the Training Department or somebody else's cost center, it's not viewed with nearly the same seriousness as it would be if each department or workgroup were required to fund it themselves. Better yet, why not require each employee to personally budget (and account for) their *own* development expense?

5. Finally, and perhaps most importantly, what are your training priorities?

Sounds like a stupid question, but most organizations don't have a clue. Instead, they approach the subject like a family of four in a Chinese restaurant: "Let's have one from column A, one from column B, etc." And just like the Chinese meal, when the food shows up, people eat what they like and don't eat what they don't want. The problem with this haphazard approach is that it

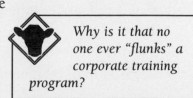

*Why is it that no one ever "flunks" a corporate training program?*

guarantees you'll spend more than you should, and you'll never get full or, in business terms, reach the critical mass which is essential to getting some return on that investment. If, for example, customer service training for front line employees is a priority, then every single front line customer contact employee ought to get it. No exceptions and no free passes! If leadership training is a priority, then every single leader ought to get it. No exceptions there, either! Just think about it. How would you like to get on an airplane knowing that the captain and first officer had opted out of their emergency cockpit procedures class?

## CHAPTER SUMMARY

Training is a vital part of the enabling process, and is a competitive advantage. Fully 90 percent of the $30 billion or so spent annually on training is spent by only 0.5 percent of all U.S. companies, with much of that being wasted. You must:

- treat training as something other than a luxury
- link it tightly to your business strategy
- know how to organize and deliver it
- set clear ROI expectations (individual as well as organizational)

### Best Practices

a. New Product Training at Crate & Barrel.
b. New employee orientation at Disney and Rosenbluth Travel.
c. Marriott's non-traditional "real world" curriculum.
d. Leadership development at GE, Southwest, and FedEx.

# ENABLED EMPLOYEES ARE TOOLED

$\left(\begin{array}{c}\text{Tooled} - \text{To equip with the}\\ \text{means for production}^1\end{array}\right)$

*In any competitive situation, a chief duty of leadership is to minimize the impact of unexpected conditions and distractions on the team in combat. This demands the trained eye, awareness, and judgment of the leader if the troops are to prevail on the battlefield.*

—Pat Riley

## TOOLS, NOT RULES

We've said this before, but it's so important, we're going to say it again: Organizations don't become *Contented Cows* purely on the strength of their employee relations practices. All of your policies, methods, systems, and procedures have an impact on your workforce in some way. So come on, broaden your concept of what makes a cow contented! It does no good to go out and hire talented people who fit well within the organization; get them all fired up about the voyage; equip them with a capable leader; and train the stew out of them, if forces within your organization's *system* are going to frustrate or prevent them from performing.

What we are talking about is analogous to going out and spending a half million dollars to build an Indy car, another half million to get a backup car, hiring a top-name driver and pit crew, paying for months of practice, then about 30 minutes before the race, sending your crew chief out to put a governor on the engine. While none of us would *plan* to do something this stupid, we somehow manage to pull it off on a fairly regular basis. We do it through policies that are just plain dumb; systems that treat intelligent people like they're complete morons; and cultures which ensure that no mistake goes unpunished.

## BE CAREFUL WHAT YOU INCENT; YOU'LL LIKELY GET IT!

At the risk of offending some of our friends in the compensation profession, most pay systems suck a big egg. They are not only broken, they make no sense. They not only fail to incent people to do their best, but in many cases, actually induce them to do a poor job.

Perhaps the most obvious example is paying someone according to how much time it takes them to do something—a notion which in nearly every case is fundamentally bankrupt. Anybody who registers an I.Q. can figure out very quickly what they need to do to make more money under such a time-based arrangement, and it's not in your customers or stockholders' interest for them to do it. So why in the world do we pay people that way? Some would have you believe that it is required by law. Not true! Companies like Worthington Industries and Chaparral Steel have known this fact for a long time; their employees are all salaried.

Be especially careful in defining what it is you motivate people to do, because that is exactly what they're *going* to do. Sears was reminded of this in the early '90s when, as the result of a new pay scheme for its automotive service people, they wound up with a public relations nightmare when the company was accused of systematically defrauding car-repair customers by making unneeded repairs.[2]

Conversely, Lincoln Electric, the Cleveland-based manufacturer of electric motors, has enjoyed immense success over its 100-plus year history, due in part to its unique piecework pay system which rewards employees for doing exactly what they're supposed to be doing. By the way, they are also afforded the opportunity to earn well in excess of area wages and to manage their own work (the foreman to worker ratio is reportedly in the neighborhood of 1:100).

All organizations would do well to scrutinize with a healthy dose of suspicion the job evaluation systems they use to determine the relative worth of each job—principally of the managerial and professional variety. Most are based on some version of a point factor system which gives credit for things like the knowledge and skill required to do the job, and the level of accountability that goes with the position. This seems a perfectly rational and reasonable approach until you consider the outdated

> *It's very likely that a substantial portion of your employees don't understand why you pay them what you do.*

means by which something like accountability is usually gauged—the size of the individual's budget and the number of people reporting to them. Here again, the goals of the organization (be more productive, effective, etc.) and those of the individual (make more money) become completely incongruent, and, over time, we know which one is going to win out.

This same argument can also be made in other areas. Based on a fairly traditional model and some rather curious logic, many organizations furnish their employees with a finite number of "sick days" each year. The intent is that these days will be used as income protection when the person is, due to unavoidable illness or injury, unable to come to work. But people feel compelled to use up their allotment of days each year, regardless of whether or not they are actually ill.

Let's compare this to two different approaches a bank could take to protect its customers against overdrafts. One approach would be for the institution to provide each customer with an additional $1,000 each year, with the caveat that the money only be used to protect against overdrafts. (We've got a feeling we know how this scenario would play out.) Or, they could advise credit-worthy customers (would they really want any other kind?) that, within reason, they would temporarily cover account overdrafts. However, the bank warns that if the customer abuses the privilege, they will have to revise the relationship, or terminate the agreement.

Companies which take this latter approach with the issue of sick days, like Chaparral Steel and FedEx, are beginning to experience significantly fewer unscheduled absences. In some cases, they are reporting unscheduled absence rates of less than 1 percent of scheduled work days versus a mean of around 1.6 percent for all employers.

Now let's assume for the moment that you've managed to get most of the dumbness out of your pay and benefit systems; that you're no longer paying anyone (including your accountant and attorney) on an hourly basis; that you're not paying people who should be cooperating with one another to compete; and that everyone's got a substantial portion of their pay at risk. We're home free, right?

WRONG! Because it's very likely that a substantial portion of your employees don't understand *why* you pay them what you do or what exactly it is they must do to make more. And they certainly can't appreciate the linkage between their reward system and the organization's overall performance (assuming there is one).

A case in point: In April 1996, the board of directors of Delta Air Lines approved a generous stock option program for their employees, granting them, on average, the right to purchase approximately 300 shares of DAL over the next 10 years.[3] The decision was based on the perceived need to generate a higher level of goal-congruence between DAL and its employees, and to pump up sagging morale. That's all well and good, except for one thing. It has now been well over a year since the program was approved, and most of their people know nothing about it. Of the 50 or so randomly selected DAL employees we spoke with, roughly 30 knew nothing about the program at all, and *none* of them were able to explain it!

## THE PROPER USE OF BONUSES

We know a fellow who runs one of the largest independent Honda auto-repair garages in America. The business is growing and thriving mainly because (get this) customers love them! Anyhow, at the end of his first full year of leadership, our friend John wanted to share some of the spoils with those who had helped make a good year possible. Despite his partners' wishes to the contrary, he instructed the company accountant to cut a generous bonus check for each employee, hoping that it would strengthen the link between individual and corporate interests.

Unfortunately, the ink was barely dry on the back of those checks when John called us with bad news. His people were no more attuned to the company or its customers than they were *before* the bonuses. He still had a contingent that came to work late every day, others who wouldn't lift a finger to help a co-worker, and, worst of all, he was seeing a noticeable decline in the performance of some of his better people.

So what was at the root of all this? Well, it seems that some of the better performers were miffed that they had fared no better than others who, by virtue of their lackluster performance, already had one foot on a banana peel. And, more importantly, no one really understood what the bonuses were for in the first place! In the final analysis, John had not only pumped a sizable chunk of his net income down a dry hole, he had actually managed to make things worse!

Sadly, this same saga is played out every day as ESOP's, 401-(k)s, profit sharing plans, and a variety of shorter-term performance incentives fail to work as well as they should because people don't understand them. The answer isn't to abandon these devices as a means of encouraging maximum effort, but rather to first ensure that they are sensibly and simply designed, and then to take the time and expend the effort necessary to ensure that people understand and appreciate them. Remember Peter Lynch's point from Chapter 4. Get out your crayons!

Still, if well-designed and implemented, incentive programs can bring productivity gains worth far more than the outlay. InTuition's David Graham credits part of his company's turnaround to an incentive bonus and profit sharing plan. Designed to be awarded for both individual *and* team performance, the team component is especially powerful. If one team member sees another slacking or doing something that will adversely affect the company's profits, he or she will exert the necessary peer pressure to correct things. "Hey, that's my bonus you're messing with!" they're likely to say. The collective efforts of all the members of the team, who know precisely how the bonus is figured, is a great motivating force.

Our advice is to keep incentive programs fresh, and relevant to the desired performance by making sure everyone knows exactly what and where the target is. "You've got to tweak them [incentive plans] from time to time," Graham cautions. "Don't let them grow stale. After a while, they lose their incentive value and start to be viewed as an entitlement."[4]

## HELP NOT HINDER

*Contented Cows* go to great lengths to develop and implement not only policies, but procedures and support systems which are designed to make heroes (not scapegoats) out of their employees, most particularly those who serve on the front line.

Marriott discovered an example of this in some of its hotel property restaurants. It seemed that the wait staff on the breakfast shift was spending something like 70 percent of their time doing things other than waiting on tables. When they investigated the situation further, they found their waiters and waitresses frequently having to spend time in the kitchen doing things like picking up orders, making toast, and rummaging through the freezer for new containers of juice while their customers were left wondering why the coffee refill was taking so long. Today, as the result of reworking the support system at some Marriott properties, *the servers never even have to enter the kitchen*. The culinary staff takes care of all food preparation.

**MARRIOTT INTERNATIONAL, INC. OPERATING PROFIT**

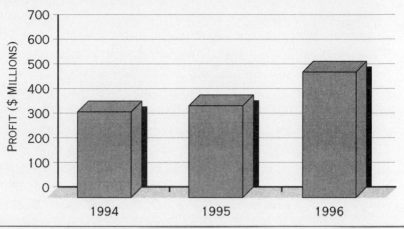

*Source:* Marriott International Annual Report, 1996.

When a meal is ready, the kitchen beeps the server and a runner delivers it to the table for presentation by the server.[5]

## OVERBOOKED ON THE INTERNET

Contrast Marriott's handling of their problem with the first great cyber-fiasco of the internet industry. You know the one we mean: America Online. In December of 1996, AOL switched to an unlimited usage plan with most of its eight million subscribers. The only trouble was that the company failed to prepare—to equip itself—with adequate capacity to handle the switch from measured to unlimited service. And so millions of subscribers found it impossible to sign onto the system except in the dead of night. This was, as one analyst put it, like selling 10,000 tickets to a concert in a hall that only seats 800.

How would you like to be an AOL telephone customer service representative in the midst of this debacle? All you can do is sit there with egg on your face and take it—endure every call—because, you know what? Every one of those angry customers is right.

## NO SALE ON COLD TURKEY

Two weeks before Christmas one year, the microwave oven in my house started malfunctioning. Now, I don't know about your place, but that's about the last thing we want to live without during the holiday season. So I called 1–800–949–7185, home of the people whose repair vans are emblazoned with the words "We Service All Major Brand Name Appliances No Matter Where You Bought Them," and whose yellow-pages ad proudly states, "Free Service Call When We Repair."

After the usual identification process with the telephone representative, I stated the problem: Something was causing the microwave to arc and burn up the turntable support. She said they would be able to come out the next day and repair the oven, and that the service call would be free, unless I chose not to have the repairs made. I indicated that was fine, but made a special point of telling her that the technician needed to be sure to bring at least a new turntable support since, for all intents and purposes, that part was toast.

Around 8:30 the next morning, the technician called to verify that someone would be home and let us know that he would arrive between 10:30AM and noon. Great! I reminded him that, at a minimum, he would need to bring a turntable support for the microwave.

The technician arrived as scheduled and immediately diagnosed the problem: "Your turntable support is defective and it's causing the thing to arc." In that moment, I was feeling pretty good for having correctly guessed the cause of the problem. I figured I'd be a hero to my family when they got home because the microwave would be fixed—Wrong! The next words out of the technician's mouth were, "I don't have that part on the truck so may I use your phone to see if we have it in stock?" My chin dropped.

Making the call he should have made four hours earlier, the technician was promptly put on hold for an eternity by his own parts department. When he finally got through, it was only to find out they didn't have the part, would have to order it, and even if they put a "rush" on it, I'd be "looking at a minimum of seven–10 days with no micro." I indicated that was a bit more cold turkey than I was interested in eating, and with the technician still standing in the kitchen, picked up the phone, called the manufacturer, and ordered it myself—with a four-day committed delivery. After hanging up the phone, I turned around and the technician presented me with a bill for $40. "What's this?" I sputtered.

"Well, you refused the repair."

"No, I didn't refuse the repair; you didn't do what both you and your telephone rep were asked to do, and as a result, couldn't and didn't repair anything." Now, don't get me wrong, the fellow was very nice. In fact, while he was waiting for the parts people to wake up, we had a most enlightening conversation about what it's been like working for Sears. He was a 14-year employee and a happy camper. When asked what he liked most about his job, he responded, "They don't put any pressure on you." No, I thought to myself, they don't, but I'm about to. Following a very civil conversation in which he agreed that he could see my point, the man indicated that it wasn't up to him to tear up the invoice. Now what's wrong with this scenario?

First, the technician bears some responsibility for not acting on the information he was given at 8:30AM. Beyond that, his employer (the "softer side" people) utterly failed him, and every other repair person they have on the streets by:

1. Not backing them up with a parts ordering process which would prevent them from sitting around forever in a customer's home with a phone stuck in their ear.
2. Not trusting a 14-year employee who drives around in a $20,000-plus company vehicle equipped with at least some parts and equipment with enough latitude to make the decision on a lousy $40 repair charge.

The reflexive thing to do would be to recommend some empowering for this guy. But that's really not what's required at all. If anything needs to be empowered, it is his *job*. It should be redefined in broad enough terms that it requires him (and everyone like him) to do more than just show up when he's supposed to, be polite, and make an honest effort to repair an appliance. Rather, it should be his job to first fix *me*, the customer, and then do whatever it takes to get the appliance squared away. There is a big difference.

The moral of my micro experience: As you continue trying mightily to get your people to take ownership for their jobs and make customers their own, you've got to realize that the *only* way that's going to happen is by enabling them to succeed. Otherwise, it's going to be business as usual. It will continue to be *your* job and *your* customer. And the employee will continue to "just fix microwaves."

## NO-FAULT MAIL ORDER

Now, contrast that example of a disempowered appliance repairman on a house-call with an enabled computer repair technician on the phone a thousand miles away. I placed an order in January 1995 with Mac and PC Connection*, the mail-order computer people in Marlow, New Hampshire. I was delighted when an express delivery truck showed up the next day with a box containing my new computer system. Everything was great until I booted up and the screen started flickering, and kept flickering. Within two minutes of placing a call to the company, I was speaking with Ann, a repair technician, who walked me through some basic diagnostics and one rather simple repair attempt. It didn't work.

At this point Ann apologized for my problem (even though she didn't make the computer), and asked if it would be okay if they shipped a replacement to me that evening, for delivery the next morning. "Don't you need to check with somebody before you ship me another $2,500 computer, particularly since you won't even have this one back yet?" I asked. She responded, "No

---

* Since its founding in 1982, PC Connection has brought mail order out of the dark ages. The company has won PC World's "World Class Award for Best Mail Order Company" an unprecedented six times, and was named by the Boston Computer Society as "Best All-Around Company" in the entire computer industry. They are New Hampshire's largest private employer.[6]

sir, I can see you've done business with us for a while, and that won't be necessary at all. I'm just sorry you had the problem. As soon as you're able, pack up the defective machine, call us, and we'll have it picked up."

Wanna make a bet which employee went home happier that night, and which companies' business prospects are brighter?

## THE MEANING OF MISTAKES

3M is a *Contented Cow* which knows a thing or two about making mistakes. With 50,000 different products on the market, and an internal requirement that 30 percent of each year's sales must come from products less than four years old, they've undoubtedly experienced lots of missteps along the way. They realize that the relentless pursuit of innovation is anything but a straight path.

In "Philosophy of Management," a paper published in 1941, former 3M President William L. McKnight explained the company's approach. *Those men and women to whom we delegate authority and responsibility, if they are good people, are going to want to do their jobs in their own way. ... Mistakes will be made, but if a person is essentially right, the mistakes he or she makes are not as serious in the long run as the mistakes management will make if it is dictatorial and undertakes to tell those under its authority exactly how they must do their job. Management that is destructively critical when mistakes are made kills initiative, and it is essential that we have people with initiative if we are to continue to grow.*[7]

## MISTAKES MUST ABSOLUTELY, POSITIVELY NOT GO UNPUNISHED

We said early on that we're not holding the *Contented Cows* out as models of perfection. Occasionally they, too, step in some cow chips. Our impression, though, is that they are very fleet of foot at recognizing and learning from their mistakes.

An example: Throughout much of the '80s, the nature and characteristics of the average package tendered to FedEx changed. Packages became smaller, lighter in weight, and, in ever increasing numbers, contained vital correspondence rather than goods and materials. The company responded beautifully with the successful marketing of the now ubiquitous FedEx Letter. However, with the dizzying growth in letter volume came some new and different operating problems.

One of the more vexing problems resulted from the size and dimensions of the Overnight Letter envelope (as it was then known) and its propensity for getting lost in the back of the company's delivery vans. As they went about the process of picking up packages throughout the day, the company's couriers would return to the van, put the freight in the back, and drive off to their next stop. Over the course of the afternoon, these loose packages—and in particular the Overnight Letter envelopes—had a nasty habit of sliding around and finding their way into small crevices in the cargo section. This made them invisible to the couriers when they unloaded the truck at the end of the day.

The net result was that the overlooked letters remained in the van overnight (or perhaps several nights) before being discovered, and customers in increasing numbers weren't getting what they had paid for. At the time, the company had somewhere in excess of 30,000 couriers and carried approximately one million packages per night, roughly half of which were Overnight Letters. It doesn't take a rocket scientist to figure out that the potential magnitude of the problem was huge, and that on any given day, a lot of packages were practically begging to be misplaced!

Despite all the things they've done well over the years, FedEx management reacted in an uncharacteristically shortsighted manner. Taking the position that these overlooked packages were obviously the result of a careless or uncommitted workforce, their solution was to impose formal, written disciplinary action in any (and every) situation where a package was overlooked. The warning letters soon began to pile up by the hundreds, giving birth to new expressions "leave a letter, get a letter" and over time, these reprimands actually became something of a status symbol. In the eyes of many couriers, you were nobody unless you had at least one written warning.

But it was no laughing matter because, in the process, a lot of otherwise good employees lost their jobs due to an accumulation of warning letters. (FedEx believed in the three-strikes-and-you're-out approach). Moreover, the overlooked-package problem not only didn't get better, it got worse! Some couriers may or may not have been lazy, but they certainly weren't stupid. With foreknowledge of exactly what would happen if they ever did discover an overlooked package in the back of their van, many took direct measures to ensure that no such package was ever discovered. It wasn't until the company backed off the *every mistake will be punished* approach and began actively soliciting courier ideas that this problem started getting solved.

> *The hustlinest team makes the most mistakes.*
> —John Wooden, legendary UCLA basketball coach

## GOOD-FAITH MISTAKES VS. ERRORS OF THE HEART

Our research and experience suggest that the *Contented Cows* (including FedEx) have done a better-than-average job of reducing the level of fear within their organizations. *Contented Cow* companies, like Hewlett-Packard, reduce fear by putting in place systemic measures to minimize the possibility of arbitrary treatment; by taking a longer view of the expected length of the employment relationship; and by permitting (and even encouraging) their people to actively experiment *and* make some mistakes.

They distinguish, however, between the types of mistakes that busy people are inclined to make when they're really leaning forward and doing their best to produce, versus the "errors of

> *They distinguish, however, between the types of mistakes that busy people are inclined to make when they're really "leaning forward" and doing their best to produce, versus the "errors of the heart."*

the heart" where a person has knowingly violated one of the organization's core precepts. In the latter case, they don't suffer sin-
ners very well. In fact, they don't tolerate them at all. David
Packard made it known early on that anyone (repeat, anyone)
who violated HP's ethical principles in order to increase short-
term profits would be fired, without exception.

## "I DON'T HAVE BIGOTS ON MY PAYROLL"

The same can be said for FedEx's Fred Smith. At one point in the
late '70s, during the company's peak growth years, a station manager was having a difficult time getting a bill paid by the accounts
payable department in Memphis. At the time, *everyone* in the
company was having trouble getting bills paid because there still
wasn't a lot of money floating around, and development of the
corporate infrastructure (A/P, A/R, Payroll, and the like) lagged
the revenue systems by a wide margin.

During the course of a phone conversation with an A/P clerk,
the manager apparently uttered a racial epithet. Word of the inci-
dent quickly reached Smith, who reportedly picked up the
phone, called the manager personally, and asked him if he had
indeed made the remark. The man was big enough to admit that
he had, whereupon Smith informed him that, "It sounds to me
like you're a bigot, and I don't have bigots on my payroll." Click.

## CHAPTER SUMMARY

Tooling is, in effect, the process of ridding your organization of success inhibitors—those things which serve as barriers to people either doing the right things, or doing things right. Some examples:

- Policies that are antiquated or just plain dumb.
- Practices that frustrate rather than support personal effort.
- Systems (e.g., pay) which encourage or even reward people for doing the wrong things.
- Failed communication methods which guarantee that nobody understands anything!

1. You must discern between good faith mistakes and "errors of the heart."

2. Make sure your pay and incentive systems are not only well designed, but also well communicated.

**Best Practices:**

a. Salaried Workforces at Worthington Industries and Chaparral Steel.
b. Lincoln Electric's "piecework pay system."
c. InTuition's Team Incentives.
d. Marriott's redesigned table service.

# ENABLED EMPLOYEES ARE TRUSTED

*People below the acme of the corporate pyramid trust those on top about as far as they can throw a Gulfstream IV, with shower.*

—Alan Farnham

In *Fortune*'s December 1989 issue cover story, Alan Farnham detailed in an all-too-sobering way what he terms the Trust Gap that is eating away at corporate America. The article focused on employees' general mistrust of their management. It just as easily could have focused on the other side of the trust equation, namely the degree of trust organizations were vesting in their people. Think about it. ...

In their private lives outside of work, your employees are heads of families, civic leaders, army reserve officers, mortgage holders, and a host of other things. Day in and day out they somehow manage to feed themselves and their families, pay their bills on time, stay out of jail, and behave normally by most reasonable standards. In short, they tend to be rather competent individuals with a clear picture of the difference between right and wrong.

Why then, when at work, must they face a continual barrage of not-so-subtle signs of our mistrust in them as individuals? Institutionally, we seem to find new ways every day to treat them like children, or worse. Not so, you say? Well, consider this: If you offered to pay a neighbor's child to pick up some groceries for you at the store (say, a couple of steaks, a loaf of bread, a carton of eggs, and some *Contented Cow* Milk), when they returned with the groceries would you:

- ask to see their time card, signed by a parent or supervisor,
- check their odometer readings and the price tag on each item,
- read them your eight-page policy on grocery purchases,
- march them through a metal detector at your front door,
- double count your change,
- demand a receipt?

We didn't think so. Now, if you're not going to ask for such an accounting from the kid down the street, what reason is there for requiring it of someone who has presumably passed your panel interview process, had their employment and criminal references checked, completed a personality profile, and successfully peed in a bottle? *After all, this is someone you have an opportunity to observe working for eight hours a day.*

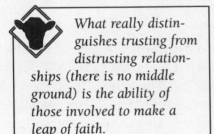

*What really distinguishes trusting from distrusting relationships (there is no middle ground) is the ability of those involved to make a leap of faith.*

Trust. Integrity. Call it what you will. But whether it's as a customer, supplier, or employee, it is one of the key factors which differentiates the *Contented Cows* from the also rans. In our view, what really distinguishes trusting from distrusting relationships (there is no middle ground) is the ability of those involved to make a *leap of faith*. They must believe that each is interested in and committed to the other's welfare, and that neither will act without first considering the impact on the other.

## NORDSTROM TRUST—AS SIMPLE AS IT GETS

Nordstrom, the Seattle-based department store, has become synonymous with legendary customer service. Something must be working, because in a cutthroat industry with competitors entering (and exiting) the market almost every day, this company enjoyed a 139 percent rate of sales growth from 1987 to 1995.[1] Patrons keep coming because what everybody says about Nordstrom is true—they have outstanding customer service (and fine merchandise as well).

One clue as to how they're able to get their 42,000 employees to render such outstanding service can be seen in the *Nordstrom Employee Handbook*. We've reproduced the complete and unabridged text below:

---

### WELCOME TO NORDSTROM

*We're glad to have you with our company.*

*Our number one goal is to provide outstanding customer service.*

*Set both your personal and professional goals high. We have great confidence in your ability to achieve them.*

**Nordstrom Rules:**

*Use your good judgment in all situations.*

*Please feel free to ask your department manager, store manager or division general manager any question at any time.*

**Nordstrom**[2]

---

Unlike so many of the rest of us, Nordstrom apparently believes they made the right choice at the outset—by hiring adults with some modicum of good sense and judgment. The handbook, which allows them to treat their people as mature, competent professionals, is simply an extension of that faith.

## REAL GOOD FAITH BARGAINING

In January 1995, the pilots of Southwest Airlines signed an unheard-of 10-year contract with the company. The contract was remarkable not only because of its length, but also the fact that it froze wages for the first five years in exchange for stock options. Said Southwest Executive Vice President Gary Baron, "To me, the bigger thing was the level of trust that had to exist between management and the employee group. … It's not just the money … they signed a contract which froze work rules in place for that 10-year period because they believe that we are willing, if things change dramatically, to change something if it needs to be changed."[3]

Trust tends to be based as much on the personal (i.e., manager-employee) relationship as it is on the policies and practices of the institution at large. Even in organizations where some very bad things are going on, one can still find pockets of high morale and productivity. In some respects, it may be similar to the underpinnings of motivation long understood and taught by the military. Chiefly, the notion that when push comes to shove, people don't fight for the flag, or mom, or apple pie; they fight for the guy who's standing next to them. Their trust is based not on symbols or feelings, but reality.

## RETHINKING THE BREAK ROOM

Trust is demonstrated in so many small, seemingly infinitesimal ways. At SAS Institute, for instance, they apparently believe that "well-fed cows give better milk." Every floor of each of the 18 buildings on its sprawling Cary, North Carolina, campus has a well-stocked break room with a veritable cornucopia of stuff to eat and drink. Everything from crackers to M&Ms, all paid for by the company.[4] Everyone is trusted to consume only what they want. There's nothing to stop someone from shoving three boxes of Cracker Jacks in their bag and schlepping them home for those nights when they've got the munchies. Well, maybe there is. Perhaps it's the fact that they're trusted not to.

Remembering a former job, SAS Institute co-founder and President Jim Goodnight recalled, "We had guards at the door every day. We had to sign in. You'd go down the hall and put your quarter in the machine and get a cup of coffee out. A lot of those things I found somewhat offensive." Determined to create a different type of organization, Goodnight maintains, "If you do right by people, they'll do right by you."⁵

Let's not be naive. There are some untrustworthy characters out there, and a few others who, for whatever reason, just don't get it. For those, our advice is simple. Get rid of them, NOW, or whenever and wherever they pop up. The answer is *not* to try to bring them into line by enacting dumb policies and other measures which do little more than frustrate the efforts of hundreds of capable, hard working, honest people who are simply trying to get their work done. It just won't work. The only thing you're going to get from spending precious time and energy building bigger and better mousetraps is smarter mice. Or, as FedEx founder Fred Smith is fond of saying, "We're not going to lower the river—we can only raise the bridge."

> *The only thing you're going to get from spending precious time and energy building bigger and better mousetraps is smarter mice.*

HP's David Packard recounted just such an example from his work at GE in Schenectady in the '30s. "The company was making a big thing of plant security. GE was especially zealous about guarding its tool and parts bins to make sure employees didn't steal anything. Faced with this obvious display of distrust, many employees set out to prove it justified, walking off with tools or parts whenever they could. Eventually GE tools and parts were scattered all around town, including the attic of the house in which a number of us were living. In fact, we had so much equipment up there that when we threw the switch, the lights on the entire street would dim."⁶ In later years, Packard and HP cofounder, Bill Hewlett, took pains to ensure that their company learned from GE's mistakes by insisting that lab storerooms remain unlocked. Said Packard, "The open bins and storerooms were a symbol of trust, a trust that is central to the way HP does business."⁷

## A GOLD-MEDAL EFFORT

Just prior to the 1988 Olympic Winter Games held in Calgary, Canada, an official of the Dutch Olympic Team went to his local FedEx Account Executive in Amsterdam with a problem. It seemed that team officials had somehow failed to file the necessary registration papers with the IOC, and unless the documents were delivered in Calgary by midnight the following day, the team would be denied the opportunity to participate in the Games.

While FedEx service is good, the A/E knew that the very best they could do at that time with a westbound trans-Atlantic package was going to take one day too long, so he took it upon himself to purchase a plane ticket and personally deliver the important document. He didn't ask anyone's permission, he just did it.

Now some might argue that what this young man did was terribly wasteful. And if the only thing taken into account was this one transaction, they would be right. After all, he had spent a couple days of his time and several hundred dollars of the company's money on a package that might have been worth $50 in revenue. But that's not the point. It wasn't then, and it's not now.

What is important is that when faced with the opportunity to solve a customer's problem, he acted. Over the course of his career, this fellow will no doubt have hundreds of opportunities just like this one. Armed with the reassurance that his boss and the company have faith that he will do the right thing, he'll continue to act in the customer's interest, and, in the vast majority of cases, he's going to get it right.

> [Southwest Airlines founders Rollin King and Lamar Muse] allowed employees to do whatever it took to get the job done. They didn't stand over us with a whip and say, "I want this done this way."[8]
> —Dennis Lardon, Southwest Airlines director of flight attendants

## TRUST KEEPS THINGS RUNNING UP TO SPEED

A central message flashing insistently from all the *Contented Cow* companies has to do with speed. At FedEx, it's the very essence of their business. As founder Fred Smith is accustomed to saying, "All we are is a 550-mile-per-hour warehouse." Southwest runs circles around its competition by being able to open a station in a new city faster than anyone else and turn its planes in less than half the time it takes competitors. GE's Jack Welch frequently comments, "If you're not fast, you're dead." 3M's insistence on coming out with massive numbers of new products at an ever increasing rate is another good example.

Speed is no accident, and it can *only* be accomplished by a workforce which is free to act because they are trusted, rather than having to ask for permission all the time. Motivated people move faster.

In his book, *Moments of Truth*, Jan Carlzon points out that employees must be afforded unquestioned authority to act in the customer's behalf. If they must stop to seek permission, more often than not, the opportunity will be forever lost. More important even than the immediate impact on the individual customer is the long term effect those situations have on the employee involved.

Lands' End tells its 3,500 employees that "they can do whatever they think they need to do to take care of a customer." In a similar vein, they do not restrict employee access to their giant warehouse via security guards, ID badges, and all the usual stuff. Says President and CEO Mike Smith, "Our culture is a critical part of who we are. It's our competitive advantage. If we maintain that, we'll be successful. If we lose it, we become a different company."⁹

> *The aim here is not so much to make people feel powerful, but rather, to keep them from feeling powerless.*

The aim here is not to make people feel power*ful*, but to keep them from feeling power*less*. When a person feels prohibited from using their own judgment, their sense of responsibility for

## LANDS' END NET INCOME PER SHARE

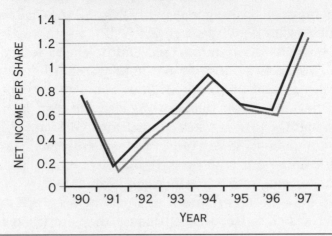

*Source:* Lands' End Financial Report (unaudited), First Quarter, 1997

the situation around them quickly evaporates and the not-my-job syndrome takes over.

Even tiny amounts of discretionary authority will ward off the energy sapping helplessness and despair that people feel when they find themselves dominated by forces beyond their control. This represents anything but a soft-touch management approach; it fosters greater rather than lesser expectations of people. Allowing the lions to manage their own den is a far cry from asking or expecting them to run the whole zoo!

## RAISE DISCRETIONARY AUTHORITY AND SPENDING LIMITS

One of the first areas to look at is the amount of discretionary authority you vest in your employees. Get them involved (as Hewlett-Packard has done) in the hiring process, not as mere bystanders, but as decision makers. Better yet, put them in charge of it. Involve them in promotional decisions, most particularly those involving front-line management positions. Put them in charge of manpower scheduling. Permit them (no, *require* them) to be personally involved in and responsible for some spending decisions. Levi Strauss, for example, has been known to involve its forklift drivers in the purchasing of new forklift trucks.

At a minimum, afford them unquestioned authority (literally) to commit an amount of resource equivalent to at least one week's pay to improve their ability to do their jobs, or to satisfy a customer. Managers (or team-based units) operating with their own cost center or P&L should have at least four to five times that much discretionary authority.

Steve Wynn, CEO of Mirage Resorts, takes it even further. "We tell our people, 'If you see a hotel guest with the tiniest frown on her face, don't ask a supervisor, take care of it. Erase the charge, send the dinner back, don't charge for the room.' "[10]

Not unlike Southwest and Suburban Propane (under Dennis Spina's leadership), companies which demonstrate high levels of trust frequently see trust reciprocated on a massive scale when employees instruct their unions to accept less restrictive work rules, or they throw the union out altogether.

> *If you assign people heavy responsibilities, that implies confidence in them, and belief in their ability to deliver the goods. Such a move stimulates their desire to prove your faith is well-founded.*[11]
>
> —Price Pritchett

## MAKE THAT IN SMALL DENOMINATIONS, PLEASE

In *INC* Magazine's September '96 issue, Editor George Gendron passed along an all-too-real corporate horror story. It seems that a distinguished looking man wearing jeans visited a bank branch one day. He was advised that the person who needed to assist him with his transaction was unavailable, and that he should return at a later time. Upon getting this news, he asked the teller to validate his parking receipt. When he was told "no, the validation can occur only in conjunction with a transaction," he rather firmly asked that it be done anyhow. Again he was rebuffed with the explanation that it was bank policy "only to validate parking for customers who had a transaction with the bank." At this point, the man satisfied the bank's requirement for a transaction by withdrawing the million or so he had on deposit.[12]

This teller must have demonstrated *some* intelligence when she was hired to work for the bank, right? What turned this person into a complete idiot between the day she was hired and the fateful day the man wanted to do business with the bank? A lack of trust, embodied in and promulgated via an unintentionally dumb corporate policy. Why do costly lessons this simple have to be learned and relearned every day?

If you're unwilling to give credence to the employer/employee covenant by taking this important step, then by all means save your time, money, and breath. Go out and hire dummies whenever your company has a job vacancy, pay them as little as possible, and don't even think about training them—just hire a supervisor to stand guard over every two to three people.

*Powerlessness corrupts. Absolute powerlessness corrupts absolutely.*
—Rosabeth Moss Kanter, Harvard Business School

## CHAPTER SUMMARY

Trust is the habit of letting go, really letting go, Without trust, you will be doomed to an unacceptably slow pace. It is neither one-dimensional nor negotiable.

1. Do away with systemic signs of distrust (eg; policies, probation periods, time clocks, locked supply cabinets, etc.).

2. Dramatically increase levels of discretionary authority.

3. Remember, the aim is not to make people feel power*ful*, but to keep them from feeling power*less*.

4. Deal swiftly (and harshly) with those who "break faith," but do it individually.

**Best Practices:**

a. Southwest Airlines long-term pilot contract.

b. Steve Wynn's (Mirage Resorts) blanket approval to fix the customer's problem.

c. Open access at Hewlett-Packard, Lands' End.

d. SAS Institute's complimentary break room.

e. Nordstrom's employee handbook.

*Employees with integrity are the ones who build a company's reputation. Working for the Coca-Cola Company is a calling. It's not a way to make a living. It's a religion.*[13]

—Roberto Goizueta

# WHEN THE COWS COME HOME

## (SPECULATIONS ON THE NEAR FUTURE)

*At Southwest, the internal customers—the employees—are treated just like the external customers expect to be treated. Most of the time I would rather be at work than at home or doing other things.*
—Kara Harris – Southwest Airlines Reservations Agent

## THE CONTENTED COWS ... WHAT NEXT?

We've put a little pressure on the six *Contented Cow* companies (and a lot more on ourselves) by holding them out as beacons for others to follow. Their reputations are what they are, and we happen to think they're well deserved. Yet, will they and their shareholders continue to enjoy the advantages they've created? Will they continue to live up to and redefine what it takes and what it means to be a *Contented Cow*? Only time will tell.

Not long ago, I spent about half an hour with a fellow named Steve. For years, he has been the "greeter" at my local Wal-Mart, the same store where I met Lisa in pursuit of the watch battery. Typical of many of the company's greeters, he's a retired gentleman augmenting his pension by working at Wal-Mart. As a senior citizen who has been around the block more times and learned a lot more than most of us, I was interested in getting his perspective on the company, both as a place to work and a place to do business.

In general, Steve gave the company favorable reviews on both counts. "It's still a great place to work," he said, "but you know, it's just not the same." When pressed for some clarification about what he meant, he added that in recent years he had seen a number of subtle but, to him, significant signs of change, and not altogether for the better. "For the most part, it's little things," he said, pointing to a section of floor which should have been cleaner, and then to a couple of burned out ceiling lights. "Mr. Sam wouldn't have liked that."[1]

To Steve and other Wal-Mart associates we talked with in different stores, there were signs of erosion they attributed to the passing of the baton that occurred after Sam Walton's death. But, in fairness to Wal-Mart CEO David Glass, there will never be another Sam Walton.

FedEx is no more immune than Wal-Mart—*or any other company*—to the inexorable decline that can and will begin the very moment they take their eye off the ball. Unlike at Wal-Mart, FedEx founder, Chairman, and CEO Fred Smith is still very much alive, well, and in the driver's seat. Yet, his company is also showing signs that some of the bloom may be coming off the rose. Since 1989, FedEx has experienced an inordinate rise in management turnover, much of it at senior levels. Some, no doubt were pushed, but many weren't.

Several insiders we know have suggested that the company's defining values (expressed by the People-Service-Profit moniker) have been allowed to get a little out of sync. Many have cited as a case in point the all-too-public acrimony associated with the decision of FedEx pilots to unionize. Given his fondness for the crew workforce, this move had to have pained Smith greatly. Some have blamed this turn of events on the company's 1988 decision to acquire Flying Tigers, a company with its own storied (and radically different) culture. Regardless of the reasons, if and when FedEx starts to "lose it," the effects will be felt "in the streets" long before they're noticed "on the street." Your courier will lose a step or two and a little bit of his smile; the phones won't get answered until the fourth or fifth ring; and the trucks won't be quite as clean. You'll know.

## THE PATH AHEAD

To become *Contented Cows*, companies must realize that just as *they* have choices, their employees (particularly the better, more skilled ones) do, too. The new rules of the game have been set, and now it's only a matter of time before everyone learns how to play, and play it to their advantage.

Employees will adjust, for example, to their new-found responsibility for their work, careers, and future, and that's good. It's about time. But those organizations that can't resist returning to their paternalistic ways, or won't furnish their folks the information they need to make valid decisions about their future, will face real difficulty. Any parent who has watched a child go from the teen years to adulthood knows precisely how this goes. We must either continue to change the nature of the relationship, putting it on ever more adult-type footing, or watch helplessly as they run off and leave *us*.

We will soon evolve to having three, maybe four different classes of employees, each with varying degrees of connectedness to the organization, and totally different pay and benefit schemes. Who winds up in what class of job, and for how long and under what conditions will be a choice made as often by the employee as it is by the organization. And, lest there be any doubt about it, that choice will be made for selfish reasons.

The implications of just-in-timing and the externalization of the workforce will be profound. To the extent that we find ourselves employing contractors, temporary workers, or part-timers in *core* activities, we must find new ways of harnessing or positioning their effort as a distinct competitive advantage. Otherwise, everyone winds up working for Manpower and, along with things like loyalty, dedication, and willingness to part with discretionary effort, the advantage goes away.

## NO MORE BIG BROOMS OR SILVER BULLETS

Managers have received a break over the past several years. The "big brooms" of downsizing and rightsizing have enabled us to gracefully disguise the firing of non-performers and malcontents.

We were able to push them out the door with everybody else, and do it with a lot less commotion and unpleasantness than if it had happened on a case-by-case basis. But the big brooms are becoming silent. Thankfully, Lean and Mean has pretty well run its course. There aren't too many companies left with a need to undergo the kind of radical restructuring we've seen over the past decade, and besides, Al Dunlap has got a job now (*just kidding, Al*).

Given the heightened criticality of *everyone* on our payroll, we must do a much better job of facing up to performance issues. Performance appraisal and the whole PIP process will become of paramount importance. Let's face it, this is something we've done a miserable job with in the past! The Deming crowd would have us believe that we should just do away with the process; but with all due respect, they're wrong. It's an issue far too important to simply shrug our shoulders and run away from. We've got to figure it out, and do it sooner rather than later.

Professional basketball coach Pat Riley dealt with the subject head on in his book, *The Winner Within*. "Avoiding the solution of a tough, miserable problem is not discretion. It's cowardice. And it's robbery. Because as long as a serious problem goes unsolved, no team, no person can exploit its full potential. Any coach who doesn't kick the complacent ass on his team will wind up kicking his own before long."[2]

## WHAT FOLLOWS THE GOLD WATCH AND GOLDEN HANDCUFFS?

Managers will have to work harder than ever to make their organizations attractive places to work. We can't just announce the end of job security, for example, without explaining what we'll put in its place. If we can't or won't offer security, we're going to have to offer real challenge, and *lots* of freedom to pursue it. The good news is that people really *do* thrive on challenge and achievement, both of the team and personal variety. But it's going to be up to us to invent the game and erect the scoreboard.

We applaud the fact that many corporations have gone to great lengths to get their people feeling like owners. That's what it's all about. Quite a few have pursued a path of actually making them owners via stock options, grants, and the like. That's even better. But as in the example mentioned earlier involving Delta, few have communicated it very well. And even fewer have bothered to clearly articulate anything about the vagaries of the market and the occasional effects this little thing called gravity has on it. Many of us have already experienced first hand the diminishing motivational ROI one gets from "under water" stock options. What makes us think our people will feel any different?

While we needn't build an entire town as Milton Hershey did, the issue of benefits must be resolved. As the Committee for Economic Development's Frank Doyle pointed out, "Neither we nor our workers can well afford the incongruity between having a more flexible workforce and our antiquated benefit structures."[3] Moreover, in the case of healthcare benefits in particular, we must be mindful that we're within a few short years of having an entire generation of baby boomers starting to fall apart physically at an ever-increasing rate; and all this at a time when more and more of them will be without any health coverage. Whether those people are "real employees" in the traditional sense, contract workers, or something else, is immaterial. As Robert Owen figured out, if they're sick, hurt, or busted up, they can't work!

## So What About You?

In as compelling a way as we know how, we've tried to illustrate the distinct and valuable advantages of treating people right. If nothing else, maybe what we've done will confirm for your head what your heart has known all along. With just the 12 companies we chose to profile in the *Contented Cow* comparison, one group ended up with 10 extra "zeros" behind their net income figures, along with a sizable revenue growth advantage. How much more incentive do you need?

It is our fervent hope that some of the facts or ideas we've communicated will become a cause for action. But if you intend to change some of your managerial behaviors, or perhaps your outlook or assumptions—even in a small way—do it with a sense of urgency. Don't wait. Time is not your friend.

Yet, you must be deliberate. You can start by taking a no-nonsense, clear-eyed look at the way you are operating now—no copping out or scapegoating. To those who would say, "But geez, I can't really do some of these things until my boss plows the way," or "our system just won't let me, ..." we say BULL. Find a way! Go ahead without them! The truth is you can start making a difference in your company right now, without anyone's help or permission.

And just what is your company or business, anyhow? It's not the name over the door. It is not a brand, a logo, or nameplate. It isn't the products you make or services you sell. Nor is it a ticker symbol, a bank account, or a piece of paper your attorney filed in Delaware long ago.

Instead, it's the people who will (or won't) show up for work tomorrow morning, and the attitude they bring with them when they pass through the gate or front door. It's their ideas, their sweat, their emotions, their energy. It's their expectations of you and their faith in you. It's both what they are, and what they can become.

It's people who individually and collectively, but not always consciously, decide whether to:

- walk with a spring in their step or to shuffle their feet,
- smile at customers even when they're having a bad day themselves, or, to eat the customer's lunch,
- use the tools you've provided with purpose and conviction, or, take those tools home and put them in the attic,
- show up early and stay late, or, hit the snooze button, roll over, and call in sick,
- walk through fire for you, or, merely hang on well enough to avoid getting fired by you,
- say, "I can help," as opposed to, "that's not my job,"
- find a way to do it better, faster, and cheaper, or, simply settle for "good enough,"
- make something great happen here, or vote with their feet.

Again, it's a matter of choice. Yours, and then theirs. Good luck and Godspeed.

*Contented Cows DO Give Better Milk!*

## A CALL FOR CONTENTED COWS

We assume that some of you were attracted to this book by its premise and its title, and because you share a real interest in organizations that subscribe to the *Contented Cow* philosophy. We also think that the *Contented Cow* companies we've chosen to highlight are but a fraction of those organizations that have achieved financial success by treating employees well.

Do you feel your company deserves to be counted among the ranks of *Contented Cows*? If so, let us hear from you. Keep in mind, our purpose is to look at companies that recognize the commercial wisdom of treating people in certain positive ways, not those which are into social or humanitarian heroics. So, we're not looking for examples of corporate altruism, but stories of companies that have profited by creating a great place for people to work.

This is not a forum for those who are unhappy with the places they work. These stories abound, and you can hear them almost anyplace working people gather to talk, including the Web site we mentioned in Chapter 7: www.disgruntled.com.

We intend to continue our research into the whole notion of *Contented Cows* and corporate profits. If you'd like to contribute, please contact us, and do it soon.

Thanks in advance for your help.

Contented Cow Partners
4741 Atlantic Boulevard, Suite C
Jacksonville, FL 32207
904-396-9796 phone
904-396-9798 fax
http://www.contentedcows.com
e-mail: stories@contentedcows.com

# NOTES

## Introduction

1. Peters, Tom, *Thriving on Chaos* (New York: Knopf, 1987), p.286.
2. Pascale, Richard Tanner, *Managing on the Edge* (New York: Simon & Schuster, 1990), p.14.

## Chapter 1

1. Fisher, Anne B., *Fortune,* March 4, 1996, p.95.
2. Levering, Robert; Moskowitz, Milton; Katz, Michael, *100 Best Companies to Work for in America* (New York, Plume, 1984, 1985, 1993).
3. Fisher, Anne B., *Fortune,* March 4, 1996, p.F2–F7.
4. Lieber, Ronald B., *Fortune,* December 9, 1996, p.107.
5. ™Carnation Company (Nestle), used with permission.
6. Peppers, Don and Rogers, Martha, *The One to One Future* (New York, Doubleday, 1993), p.34.
7. Wright, Frank Lloyd, *An Autobiography,* second edition (Duell, Sloan and Pearce, 1943).
8. Lasorda, Tommy, *Fortune,* July 3, 1989, p.131.
9. Garfield, Charles, *Second to None* (New York, Avon Books, 1992), p.204.
10. Levering, Robert; Moskowitz, Milton; Katz, Michael, *100 Best Companies to Work for in America* (New York, Plume, 1984, 1985, 1993), p.114.
11. *Fortune,* May 12, 1997, p.106.
12. Ibid.
13. trans. Wilhelm, Richard (Ger.) and Baynes, Cary F. (Eng.), *I Ching or Book of Changes,* (New York: Pantheon [Bollingen Series XIX] 1950).
14. Engels, Frederick, *Socialism; Utopian and Scientific.*
15. Lieber, Ronald B., *Fortune,* December 9, 1996, p.107.

## Chapter 2

1. Thomas, Roosevelt, *Beyond Race and Gender* (Amacom, New York, 1991), p.14.
2. Albright, J., *Improving the Welfare of Dairy Cows Through Management* (Business and Management, 1982).
3. *The Washington Monthly,* June 1986.
4. Organ, Dennis, *Business Horizons 38, no.3* (May–June 1995).
5. Ibid.
6. Ibid.
7. Ibid.
8. Ibid.
9. Ibid.

10. Ibid.
11. National Institute on Aging Study, 1973.
12. Organ, Dennis, *Business Horizons,* May–June 1995.
13. Ibid.
14. Cathy, Truett, *It's Easier to Succeed Than to Fail* (Oliver Nelson, Nashville, 1989), p.70.
15. Johnson, Jimmy, *Turning the Thing Around* (New York, Hyperion, 1993), p.180.
16. Marriott, J. Willard, "Money, Talent, and the Devil By the Tail," *Management Review,* January 1985.
17. Reicheld, Frederick F., *The Loyalty Effect* (Harvard Business School Press, Boston, 1996), p.105.
18. Ibid, p.110.
19. Roosevelt Thomas, interview by author.

## CHAPTER 3

1. Smith, Fred W., speech at Rhodes College, February 25, 1988.
2. Mercer Management Consulting survey.
3. Pacetta, Frank, *Success,* May 1994, p.64.
4. Neuborne, Ellen, *USA Today,* December 23, 1996.
5. Garfield, Charles, *Second to None* (Avon Books, New York, 1992), p.201.
6. Neuborne, Ellen, *USA Today,* December 23, 1996.
7. Carlzon, Jan, *Moments of Truth* (Ballinger, Cambridge, MA, 1987), p.3
8. Ibid, p.95.
9. Families and Work Institute survey.
10. David Graham, interview by author.
11. Ibid.
12. Stack, Jack, *The Great Game of Business* (Doubleday, New York, 1992), p.57.

## CHAPTER 4

1. Aguilar, Francis J. and Arvind Bhambri, "Johnson & Johnson, Harvard Business School Case #384-053,4."
2. *Los Angeles Times,* December 16, 1996.
3. *USA Today,* December 23, 1996.
4. Sherman and Tichy, *Control Your Destiny or Someone Else Will* (Bantam, New York, 1993), p.245–46.
5. Freiberg, Kevin and Jackie, *NUTS* (Bard, Austin, TX, 1986), p.49.
6. Johnson, Jimmy, *Turning the Thing Around* (Hyperion, New York, 1993), p.189.
7. Lynch, Peter, *Beating the Street* (Simon & Schuster, New York, 1993), p.27.
8. Packard, David, *The HP Way* (Harper Business, New York, 1995), p.126.
9. Didinger, Ray, *Game Plans for Success* (Little Brown & Company, Boston, 1995), p.181.
10. Carlzon, Jan, *Moments of Truth* (Ballinger, Cambridge, MA, 1987), p. unnumbered.

## CHAPTER 5

1. "Business Secrets of Tommy Lasorda," *Fortune*, July 3, 1989, p.131.
2. Garfield, Charles, *Second to None* (Avon Books, New York, 1992), p.123.
3. Angela Perry, interview by author, Delta Air Lines seven-year flight attendant, met on flight #1662: July 13, 1996, seat 4-A.
4. Follett, Ken, *On Wings of Eagles* (Morrow, New York, 1983), p.63.
5. *Fortune*, October 28, 1996, p.28.
6. *Fortune*, May 3, 1993, p.37.
7. Ibid, p.36.
8. Ibid, p.41.
9. *Fortune*, October 17, 1994, p.55.
10. *Fortune*, May 4, 1992, p.58.
11. *Selling Power*, September 1996, p.64.
12. *USA Today*, May 16, 1996.

## CHAPTER 6

1. Dennis LeStrange, interview by author.
2. Adams, Scott, *The Dilbert Principle* (Harper Business, New York, 1996), p.51.

## CHAPTER 7

1. *Sky Magazine*, January 1997, p.101.
2. Ibid.
3. *Fortune*, November 11, 1996, p.201.
4. *Memphis Commercial Appeal*, December 17, 1996.
5. Westin, Alan F., and Feliu, Alfred G., *Resolving Employment Disputes Without Litigation* (BNA Books, Washington, DC, 1988).
6. Worsham, James, *Nation's Business*, June 1997, p.17.
7. *Wall Street Journal*, December 16, 1993, p.67.
8. *Wall Street Journal*, November 26, 1996, p.1.
9. *Business Week*, February 24, 1997, p.30.
10. *Worth*, June 1996, p.89.
11. *INC Magazine*, May 1996, p.21.
12. Dunlap, Al, *Mean Business* (Random House, New York, 1996), p.174.
13. Ibid, p.170.
14. Loeb, Marshall, "How to Grow a New Product Every Day," *Fortune*, November 14, 1994, p.270.
15. Smith, Fred W., speech at Rhodes College, February 25, 1988.

## CHAPTER 8

1. Johnson, *op. cit.*, p.190.
2. *Jacksonville Business Journal*, April 7, 1997.
3. Betty Kahn, interview by author.
4. *Business Week*, November 11, 1996, p.111.
5. Freiberg, Kevin and Jackie, *NUTS* (Bard, Austin, TX, 1986), p.49.

## CHAPTER 9

1. Galinsky, Ellen, *Business Week,* September 16, 1996.
2. Ibid.
3. *Compensation and Benefits Review*, January–February 1995, p.41.
4. *Best's Review, Property and Casualty Insurance Edition*, June 1996, p.16.
5. *Compensation and Benefits Review*, January–February 1995, p.41.
6. *Best's Review, Property and Casualty Insurance Edition*, June 1996, p.16.
7. Packard, David, *The HP Way* (Harper Business, New York, 1996), p.137.
8. *Best's Review, Property and Casualty Insurance Edition*, June 1996, p.16.
9. *HR Magazine*, May 1996, p.104.
10. *Training*, November 1994, p.12.
11. *HR Magazine*, May 1996, p.104.
12. Ibid.
13. Nixon, Judy, Helms, Marilyn, and White, Charles, "What Companies are Doing About Child Care," *Journal of Compensation and Benefits*, January–February 1993, p.17.
14. David Russo, interview by author.
15. *HR Magazine*, October 1994, p.79.
16. Ibid.
17. *HR Magazine*, May 1996, p.104.
18. *Human Resource Executive*, March 1996.
19. Ibid.
20. Starbucks press release.
21. *Compensation and Benefits Review*, January–February 1995, p.41.
22. Ibid.
23. Ibid.
24. Bollier, David, *Aiming Higher* (Amacom, New York, 1996), p.230.

## CHAPTER 10

1. Mintzberg, Henry, *Harvard Business Review,* July–August 1996, p.63.
2. GE 1995 Annual Report, p.3.

## CHAPTER 11

1. Packard, David, *The HP Way* (Harper Business, New York, 1996), p.135.
2. *Hoover's Company Profile Database* (The Reference Press, Inc., Austin, TX), p.4.
3. Reicheld, Frederick F., *The Loyalty Effect* (Harvard Business School Press, Boston, 1996), p.119.
4. Alford, Henry, *New York Magazine,* May 23, 1994, p.58.
5. ASTD survey, *Workplace Visions* (Society for Human Resource Management, November–December 1996).
6. Ibid.
7. Johnson, Jimmy, *Turning the Thing Around* (Hyperion, New York, 1993), p.189.
8. Betty Kahn, interview by author.
9. http://www.fed.org/uscompanies/labor/n_z/Rosenbluth_International.html (p.1)
10. *Business Week,* November 11, 1996.
11. *Fortune,* October 18, 1993, p.67.

## CHAPTER 12

1. *Merriam-Webster's Collegiate Dictionary* – tenth edition (Merriam Webster, Springfield, MA, 1993), p.1,243.
2. *San Francisco Examiner,* June 11, 1992, p.1.
3. *Delta Air Lines Proxy Statement* (September 16, 1996), p.26–27.
4. David Graham, interview by author.
5. *Fortune,* October 3, 1994, p.114.
6. http://www.pcconnection.com/about/fact.html.
7. McKnight, William L., "Philosophy of Management," 1941.

## CHAPTER 13

1. *Hoover's Company Profiles*, March 20, 1997, p.4.
2. Nordstrom Employee Handbook.
3. Freiberg, Kevin and Jackie, *NUTS* (Bard, Austin, TX, 1996), p.107–108.
4. *Sky Magazine,* October 1996, p.40.
5. Ibid.
6. Packard, David, *The HP Way* (Harper Business, New York, 1996), p.136.
7. Ibid.
8. Freiberg, Kevin and Jackie, *NUTS* (Bard, Austin, TX, 1996), p.41.
9. *Training Magazine,* October 1996, p.95.
10. *Fortune,* March 4, 1996, p.98.
11. Pritchett, Price, *Firing Up Commitment During Organizational Change* (Pritchett & Associates, Dallas, TX).
12. *INC,* September 1996, p.11.
13. *Network News*, A publication of the Coca-Cola Company, April 1997.

## CHAPTER 14

1. Wal-Mart Associate, interview by author.
2. Riley, Pat, *The Winner Within* (Putnam, New York, 1993).
3. Doyle, Frank, The Committee for Economic Development, New York, *loc. cit.*

# INDEX